Jane Bartlett was born in Southampton in 1963. She studied film and literature at Warwick University before becoming a journalist. Now a freelance, she writes for a broad range of magazines and newspapers, including *Options*, *New Woman*, *Time Out*, the *Guardian* and the *Daily Express*. She is training in psychotherapy and lives in North London.

WILL YOU BE MOTHER?

Women Who Choose to Say No

Jane Bartlett

New York University Press
Washington Square
New York

For my mother and grandmother

NEW YORK UNIVERSITY PRESS
Washington Square, New York

First published 1994 in the U.K. by Virago, London
Copyright © 1994, 1995 by Jane Bartlett
All rights reserved

Library of Congress Cataloging-in-Publication Data
Bartlett, Jane, 1963–
Will you be mother? : women who choose to say no / Jane Bartlett.
p. cm.
Includes index.
ISBN 0-8147-1244-4 (alk. paper). — ISBN 0-8147-1245-2 (pbk. :
alk. paper)
1. Childlessness—Great Britain—Case studies. 2. Motherhood—
Great Britain—Public opinion. 3. Women—Great Britain—Attitudes.
4. Choice (Psychology). I. Title.
HQ614.B46 1995
306.874'3—dc20 94-43557
CIP

New York University Press books are printed on acid-free paper,
and their binding materials are chosen for strength and durability.

Manufactured in the United States of America

10   9   8   7   6   5   4   3   2   1

Contents

Acknowledgements

I firstly want to thank all the women who kindly allowed me to interview them, and without whom this book would not have been possible. They generously gave me their time; courageously shared their inner lives, exploring the issues with vigour. So many were inspiring and a joy to talk with. I also want to acknowledge two valuable London resources for women: The Fawcett Library and The Feminist Library. Thanks also to Root Cartwright of The British Organisation of Non-Parents for his valuable suggestions and support. A special mention to journalist Marie-Françoise Golinksy for her thoughts; and journalist Karen Evenett who placed a request for interviewees in *Woman's Own* magazine. Also the friends and interviewees who 'networked' for me, hunting out child-free women who were willing to speak openly. Finally, my editor Lynn Knight, whose incisive editing skills improved my copy enormously.

Preface

FOR the first time women are speaking openly about their decision to remain child-free. Safe, reliable contraception and the opening up of paid employment are two of the major factors which have broadened possibilities for women and created the climate of choice. Motherhood has been a subject of debate since the 1970s, when the feminist movement sought to make connections between motherhood and women's political and social position. Trends in childbearing are consequently changing fast; women in Britain have fewer babies than ever before, and often delay their first pregnancy until their thirties. Most revolutionary of all, women are increasingly asking themselves whether they actually want to be mothers. According to a recent survey of 76,100 patients' records published in the *British Medical Journal*,[1] more than one in ten women is choosing not to have children, and the figure could rise to one in three. 'Despite the number of women out there without children, it doesn't get talked about much and it's a subject we've got very little information on,' says Dr Gina Johnson, one of the GPs from the South Bedfordshire Practitioners' Group which carried out the research. The doctors discovered that 15 per cent of their current female patients have no children by the age of 42 and six out of ten are yet to be mothers at the age of 25. If that generation continues as expected, up to 30 per cent of them will never give birth.

Motherhood continues to be seen as woman's highest achievement: spiritually our society exalts the ideal of motherhood based on self-sacrifice and unconditional love. Yet mothers get a very raw deal in practical terms: they are undervalued, unpaid, seen as unskilled and boring. Public and social facilities typically fail to cater for the needs of women with children. Recognising that childrearing can be as monstrous as it is wonderful, women rightly feel ambivalent. There are many books which look at what it means to be a mother, from the 'how to' baby manuals, to complex explorations of motherhood as an institution and emotional adventure. This book is intended to look at the other side of the equation and ask what it is like to *not* become a mother.

The subject of infertility is only discussed briefly here; it is covered in excellent texts elsewhere, and this is primarily a book about women who *choose* not to have children, over fifty of whom I have interviewed in depth as the essence of my research. As far as I know, it's the first study of its kind in Britain. This is emotionally loaded terrain, and one of the first problems I encountered was that of vocabulary. What do you call a woman who doesn't have children? There is no opposite word to 'mother', and 'non-mother' sounds peculiar. Similarly the word 'child-free' won't be found in any dictionary, but it's the term I use in preference to 'childless' (which implicitly suggests lack and deficiency, rather than a state reached through positive choice).[2]

This omission in our language is just one worm in a can of many: prejudice against child-free women is vehement, because like most social change, it is a slow process that meets resistance all the way. The question *why did you have children?* is rarely asked; there's an assumption that parenthood is inevitable, 'only natural' and as such is not open to query. The woman who decides not to become a mother throws all these presuppositions into confusion. People are suspicious and anxious about her. Is there something *wrong* with her? Is she selfish and materialistic? The hard-bitten career woman is a popular stereotype, or the sad spinster who pines for love. The women I interviewed all describe themselves as not having children through choice, and not one compared with either of the aforementioned stereotypes. After just twenty interviews it was very apparent that no particular 'type' of woman would emerge: all the interviewees were so completely different. They range in age from 22 to 75; they live in every region from Exeter to Fife: many are married, some are living with partners, others are single, divorced, widowed or gay. There are career high-flyers, others are factory workers and shop assistants. 'Haven't they all got dreadful family backgrounds and that's why they don't want children?' someone asked me. Well, yes, some, but equal numbers of the interviewees come from loving, secure homes, and exactly the same can be said for parents too. If there is a shared characteristic amongst the interviewees it is that they are all 'distinctive'. It takes a lot of strength and courage to swim against the tide of convention. Child psychologist and population activist Dorothy Stein admires the child-free. 'They are in general people who wish to make something interesting of their own lives and not do it vicariously through their children,' she says. I certainly found these fifty women interesting: determined, imaginative, thoughtful, loving, funny, sometimes sad, often fulfilled and happy, always spirited.

My research doesn't lend itself to detailed statistical analysis, but where facts and figures exist I've included them. As the vast majority of women do have children – 88 per cent by the age of 45 – I anticipated that it might be difficult to find sufficient interviewees who were willing to discuss such a personal issue. Here I was completely wrong. An article I wrote in the *Guardian* (15 January 1992), about a workshop for women trying to make up their mind about motherhood elicited a promising response, and these women were happy to talk further about the issues. I received a lot of help from the British Organisation of Non-Parents, a national support and campaigning group for women and men who choose not to have children. *Woman's Own* magazine was kind enough to publish a request for interviewees on its letters page. I also put up an advertisement in the Feminist Library and networked vigorously amongst friends and colleagues. The response was tremendous: in fact after ten years of seeking case histories for all manner of features as a journalist, I have never known a group of people so eager to talk about their lives. 'At last someone is going to write about us,' said one woman. 'It's good to be recognised,' said another.

Most were first interviewed through a detailed questionnaire consisting of seventy questions. It became clear that for some interviewees this was a valuable opportunity to focus clearly on their child-free choice, and the chance for introspection was undertaken with relish. Many inserted extra sheets of paper, detailing their lives in considerable depth; a few women wrote at great length. Only one woman refused to be interviewed further, describing herself as 'very ordinary with not much to say'. Each day the questionnaires fell through my letterbox, some with good luck cards enclosed, and addresses of child-free friends of the interviewees who would also like to help. Over the ensuing months I went on to interview many of the women in person, usually in their homes, or by telephone. These were either loosely structured interviews in which I tried to uncover a broader under-standing of what it means to be child-free, or directed conversations concentrating on a number of specific issues.

What interested me first and foremost were the women's stories: the complexity of the emotional journey that leads someone to make the major life decision to renounce motherhood. What are the joys and pains, losses and gains of the child-free lifestyle? How does it affect marriage and relationships? What rational and practical considerations feed into the decision-making process? I constantly endeavour to set my enquiry against a wider backdrop, looking at the social pressures exerted upon women to become mothers, attitudes towards the child-free, and historically how women have arrived at the position where they have a choice about their procreative destiny. The notion of maternal instinct is another important question that I have addressed.

This book is in no way intended to be a criticism of women who are mothers; it does not seek to undervalue the importance of the role. If anything, the child-free raise the status of parenting as they do not view it lightly; seeing it as a precious vocation that demands special qualities and skills, rather than something that anyone can do. I sincerely hope that I am breaking down barriers between women rather than building them, and believe that the fifty interviewees have as much to say to mothers as they do to women who are making up their minds, and those who have decided not to have children. Whether we like it or not, women are still principally defined in terms of their relationship to motherhood: we are all measuring our lives along that shared axis. The ground is shifting, however, and although it is still tremendously important, motherhood is increasingly viewed as one aspect of a woman's life, not its entirety. Given choice and opportunity, women want to extend their lives beyond the boundaries of maternity and seek new possibilities for themselves. Child-free women present us with different horizons and an encounter with them is liberating. They represent the fact that we are progressively free to shape our own lives because we are now able to ask ourselves: will you be mother?

1

YOU *WILL* BE MOTHER: THE SOCIAL PRESSURES TO HAVE CHILDREN

SEVERAL years ago Jane's parents acquired a beautiful old pram from a neighbour. It was one of those large Edwardian prams, in good condition and very elegant. At the time Jane, now 29 years old and a systems programmer, had just got married. Her parents wheeled the pram into the garage, and there it stood waiting for the day when she and her husband would announce the arrival of their first child. The years passed, and the pram started to gather mildew. Every time Jane visited her parents she could see it through the garage window, standing expectantly. 'It made me feel very anxious,' she remembers. 'How was I going to break the news to my parents?' Jane and her husband have decided that they do not want to have children. Such a major decision involves a lot of thought and some heart-searching, but Jane feels it's the right one for her. What she has found most difficult in reaching this decision is other people. Society expects

1

women to become mothers. Sometimes the pressure is overt, and sometimes subtle, as the giant pram silently testifies. Often we are so used to living with the pressure we do not even notice it, but like electricity it invisibly feeds into our lives. For every woman there is an awaiting pram; that immense weight of tradition that forces her into motherhood. To be able to make our own choices about parenting, it is first necessary to stand back and look closely at how we are coerced by these influences.

Myths, folklore, custom, belief, religion, social institutions, art, the media, all exalt the role of parenthood and encourage reproduction. Pressure also comes from closer sources: family and friends. To challenge this thought is to challenge what has been fundamental to our way of thinking: the view that a woman's role must necessarily involve maternity. The challenge pulls the rug out from beneath what it has always meant to be born female and confronts all the assumptions that have been made about our lives. Eventually Jane's mother sold the pram and gave her daughter the money instead. 'I think she was shocked when I said I was going to use the money to have a mural airbrushed on to my motorbike,' says Jane.

Little mothers at play

Expectations about motherhood start early and are clearly expressed. As little girls we are given dolls to play with. 'There's such a marked difference in the ways toys are aimed at boys and girls,' says David Coombs, deputy editor of the trade magazine, *Toy Trader*. 'Right from the word go, pink gets splashed across the girls' toy range, blue across the boys'. It's marketed to appeal to the parents, their opinions and views: little children don't care what colour it is.' Coombs notes that the gender divide is less in toys manufactured for the pre-school age group: 'It's only when the children get older they really gun for the two sexes. Some people just say, "Well boys like that kind of thing, the girls like that kind of thing," but by the time you get them to eight or nine, it's too late: they've already been to playgroup and been given toys by adults.'

A study of 96 middle-class homes discovered that in the 48 boys' rooms there were 375 toy vehicles: in the 48 girls' rooms there were only 17. Over half the girls possessed a baby doll, compared to just three of the boys. According to Nielsen Market Research the bestselling boy's toy in 1992 was the Matchbox car range, for girls it was the Barbie doll.

As part of a PhD at London University's Institute of Education, Jacqueline McGuire studied 40 families in an outer London borough, looking at the impact of children's gender on family relationships. She makes the following observations about toys:

> Boys' toys are predominantly vehicle and sport equipment . . . most of the toys bought for girls related to feminine activities, girls owned more than one doll, many of them baby dolls with all the necessary equipment such as buggies, baths, clothes, plus housekeeping equipment such as vacuum cleaners and cookers.[1]

Elizabeth, 26, a theatrical agent, vividly recalls the alarm she caused when she rejected playing with dolls: 'When I was a kid I'd rather be playing out in the garage with my dad's bits of wood. I had hundreds of dolls but would never play with them because they were boring. I'd rather play with my brother's cars; his toys were much more interesting. My dad didn't seem to mind, but I remember my mum once commented, "She's meant to be a girl; she's meant to be inside the house, I don't want her playing in the garage." ' Penny, 30, a graphic artist, enjoyed playing with her dolls as a child, but remembers how different her toys were from those of her two brothers: 'At Christmas they'd get all these building kits, cars and chemistry sets, very practical doing things. I'd get dolls and teddies. My toys were about forming relationships. Funnily enough, I've still got a couple of my favourite old dolls. I could never throw them away.' It's not that little girls shouldn't be *given* dolls, rather *offered* them, along with a selection of other toys which are equally emphasised. Penny feels that if she had played more with her brothers' practical toys she would be more adept with technology. 'I'm terrible with any gadgets. I've had my video for years and still haven't learnt to program it.'

Babies or workplace boredom

Despite equal opportunities legislation in Britain during the 1970s, when it comes to promotion, many women continue to be discriminated against in the workplace because there is the assumption that they will give up work to have children, and training resources will have been wasted. It's a sexist rationale that is likely to further pressurise women into motherhood: her job becomes so directionless that she will see childrearing as a more creative option and a welcome escape. In the UK women's gross weekly earnings are still only 65 per cent of men's and organisations are both horizontally and vertically segregated along gender lines. Women represent 80 per cent of hairdressers, cleaners, caterers and clerical workers, yet only 0.8 per cent of surgeons, 12 per cent of

4

solicitors, 16 per cent of secondary school head teachers and, at most, 22 per cent of managers.

Contractual maternity benefits are now a required component of an employee's package, yet guaranteed time off work for a trip to the family planning clinic or for an abortion seems unthinkable. Sex discrimination at work is a solid part of the framework that pushes women into motherhood.

Religion and motherhood

An understanding of religion and its relationship to motherhood is crucial, even for women who do not think of themselves as religious. We may think that in Britain we live in a predominantly secular culture, yet religion is fundamental to our world-view. Our values and images of ourselves, our morals and ethics all spring from a religious ethos. So too does the status of women and the fertility rate. Studies have found a significantly higher fertility rate for Muslims than non-Muslims, and in the West Catholics have higher fertility than Jews or Protestants. Religious affiliation is one of the most significant factors in determining how many children we have.

Some religions, like Catholicism, directly impose sanctions on birth control. Pope John Paul, in his 1993 encyclical, *Veritatis splendor* continues to prohibit the use of chemical or physical contraceptive methods and abortions, describing them as 'irremediably evil acts, per se, and in themselves . . . reconcilable neither with God nor the good of the person'. Abstinence or the unreliable rhythm method are the only accepted forms of birth control. Other non-Catholic Christian groups, like the Greek and Armenian orthodox churches, are less stringent:

contraception isn't categorically forbidden, although it is discouraged and abortion is opposed.

Islam has a more ambiguous position on contraception that is open to local variation. The official view taken at the first international conference on Islam and family planning held in Rabat, Morocco, in 1971 asserted the following:

> The Islamic Law ensures that the Muslim family will be able to tackle successfully any new situation and have it under control, with correct and sound solutions and measures. That the Islamic Law allows the Muslim family to be able to look after itself as regards the procreation of children. Whether this is in the sense of having many or few of them. It also gives the right to deal with sterility and to arrange suitably spaced out pregnancies, and to have recourse, when needed, to safe and lawful medical means.[2]

Of course many people do not follow all the tenets of their religion: large numbers of Catholics, for example, practise birth control to limit the size of their families.

As well as direct sanctioning, religion can indirectly affect fertility by shaping our philosophy of marriage and family, and emphasising the virtues of reproduction. According to the Catholic Church, 'large families are the most splendid flowerbeds of the Church'.[3] Christianity draws on the Old Testament's 'be fruitful and multiply'[4] philosophy. The Islamic faith regards children as a blessing from Allah, and there are references in the Qur'ān to 'marry and generate'.[5]

In an increasingly secular society, many women do not view religion as an important factor when deciding to have children. On the whole the women I interviewed expressed few religious convictions, a finding reinforced by profiles of child-free women drawn up by American psychologists who discovered that they came mainly from non-religious homes. Even Tanujah, 26, a member of Britain's Asian community where religion has a strong influence, professes no faith. 'We were brought up Jains, which is a religion close to Hinduism. I don't believe in reincarnation: when you're dead, you're dead. My parents are vegetarian, and strict Jains wouldn't eat root vegetables because of the risk of killing worms when digging them up. Now I eat meat and enjoy it.' There are, however, some exceptions: Emily, a 22-year-old student, comes from an Irish Catholic family and is convent educated. As a teenager she harboured fantasies about becoming a nun, but now lives with her boyfriend. 'I still believe in God even though I don't often go to church,' she says. 'The Catholic Church says it's wrong to waste eggs and sperm, but I think it needs to move with the times. I see no reason why I shouldn't use contraception, or why priests shouldn't get married.'

Katy, a 23-year-old administrator at a nuclear power plant, is a regular churchgoer. She and her 27-year-old husband attend a village Baptist church and have been married for two and a half years. 'I was brought up to appreciate right and wrong, my parents are nominal Christians,' says Katy. 'I became a Christian when I was 12, and then went through a rebellious adolescence. I re-committed myself to Jesus when I was 20. When I met my husband he wasn't a Christian but became one ten months later, as I couldn't have gone out with him otherwise. Initially he made a commitment to Christianity because of me, but then God really started to work and he realised he did want to be a Christian. God has guided us in our decision not to have children.'

Mention also has to be made of the 11,000 Catholic and 900 Anglican nuns in Britain, the only category of woman for whom it is socially acceptable not to have children. Nuns have a clear social role that still involves the traditional female qualities: religious sisters are seen as loving, nurturing, selfless, and somehow mothers to the populace at large. Within the convent's hierarchical structures there is even the title *Mother* Superior. Says 33-year-old Anna, an Anglican sister: 'Because we don't get married and have children people often say we've given up so much. But everyone has to give up something: a woman who becomes a mother might not be all that aware of what it's going to involve, what she's going to have to give up for motherhood. Religious sisters are human and there are difficult times for all of us because we can't get married and have children. We would be denying our humanity if we didn't acknowledge that, but it's not about what we can't do, but what we can. I'm on a journey, living in the present moment for God and each other.'

Marriage means babies

Marriage is still primarily seen as the prerequisite for starting a family. Its ceremony and rituals contain a wealth of references to offspring. The Book of Common Prayer asserts that marriage's first function is 'for the procreation of children'; sexual relations and emotional support are only 'ordained' second and third roles. The folk customs which accompany the religious tenets of marriage also stress procreation. Orange blossom and gypsophila, the flowers traditionally used in the bride's bouquet, symbolise fertility and fruitfulness, and the top tier of the wedding cake is conventionally set aside for the christening of the couple's first child.

Jane, 29, explains how the remaining tier of her wedding cake, along with the pram, has become for her parents a hopeful symbol that she and her husband will change their minds about not having children: 'My husband and I normally take a Christmas cake when we visit my parents. A couple of years ago we said we wouldn't bother buying one as we could eat the top tier of our wedding cake instead. Whenever my mother phoned us she would ask if we'd bought a cake yet, trying to preserve the wedding cake for the future. As it happens we never did get round to eating it, as we have two birthdays near Christmas and tend to get swamped with cake. However, this year I'm having it re-iced and it will be eaten at Christmas.'

Cutting down the wedding dress for the christening gown is another convention, and until quite recently it was common for mothers to keep a 'bottom drawer' for their daughters, consisting of household objects and baby items that the girl would need when she married.

The wedding itself is romantically perceived as the most important day of a couple's life. Marriage is a rite of passage that takes on fairly-tale dimensions: the voluminous white dress, bridesmaids, flowers and champagne. These happy festivities honour reproduction and parenthood: where is the celebration for the woman or man who chooses to remain single? Or the couple who choose not to marry? 'My boyfriend and I are thinking of throwing a non-wedding party,' says 29-year-old journalist Maria. She has been with her boyfriend, a personnel manager, for a year and a half and although committed to a lifelong relationship with him, does not want to marry. She feels that she too has something to celebrate along with those who choose marriage. Likewise with the christening celebration: where is the event to positively mark the fact that someone doesn't have children? These may seem ridiculous suggestions, but they serve to demonstrate how tightly woven into our culture is the pro-birth ethic. Back in 1973 an American group for the child-free, the National Organization for Non-Parents, tried to introduce a national non-parents' day, to counteract Mother's Day and Father's Day. Philanthropist and political activist Stewart Mott was voted 'non-father of the year'. 'I have observed that new fathers automatically become the centre of attention in any situation,' he wrote in the National Organization for Non-Parents newsletter. 'Non-parents have been ignored by our society, their interests and status either envied or derided. A holiday for non-parents is a symbolic expression of the fact that we, too, are human beings of worth and value and deserve a special day of recognition to contemplate and celebrate our "childfree" status.' Non-parents' Day makes a valid point, although it is perhaps silly in practice. It was a short-lived event in the States, and the organisation itself has now folded.

Images of maternity

Maternity has been idealised in art throughout history. Galleries worldwide are hung with pictures of women with baby at the breast. Literature and poetry abounds with the romance of motherhood. 'If I were hanged on the highest hill, Mother o'mine, O mother o' mine! I know whose love would follow me still, Mother o'mine, O mother o' mine,' wrote Rudyard Kipling. 'Who ran to help me when I fell, And would some pretty story tell, Or kiss the place to make it well? My Mother,' wrote Ann Taylor. The joys of motherhood are inevitably magnified, and it is unusual indeed to find art that recognises the drudgery that motherhood can mean for some.

Christianity with its idolatry of the Virgin Mary, has a unique place in Western consciousness. She is one of the subjects most frequently treated in Christian art, with the earliest examples of the Madonna dating back to AD 3. It has been suggested that the imagery developed from earlier representations of the Egyptian Goddess Isis with her son at her breast. The Byzantine world depicted the Virgin enthroned with child on her knees, or standing holding Christ in her left arm. Later, with the spread of devotional images in the late Middle Ages, there was a much greater freedom in presentations of the Virgin. Common fifteenth-century images were the Virgin of Humility, the Mother of Mercy, who shelters the faithful beneath her mantle, and the Virgin of the Seven Sorrows with seven swords driven into her heart. One of the most frequent images of the seventeenth century was the Madonna of the Rosary. More recent images have been linked to miraculous apparitions like the Madonna of Lourdes. This rich heritage of Madonna art informs much contemporary imagery of motherhood: photographs advertising nappies, the covers of baby manuals, official portraits of royalty with their newborns. The haloes may not be there, but the soft focus and incandescent lighting constantly point back to motherhood as sacrosanct. When did you ever see a Madonna changing a dirty nappy?

Although feminism has done much to expose the hardships of motherhood, the glorified love affair with family life continues in the media, where the goodness of the family is rarely questioned. The biggest-selling women's magazines are those which are family/home centred, and despite a deceptive title like *Me*, are very much about the 'Me' in relation to husband and children. When a news story is reported about a woman who has children, she is inevitably referred to as 'mother' rather than 'woman'. The most popular TV genre is the soap opera, essentially family-based drama.

In *Images of Children in American Film*[6] sociocultural film analyst Kathy Merlock Jackson explores the meaning invested in children as they appear in films. Although each decade brings with it variants according to the economic, political and social climate, the enduring representation is one of purity and faith: 'Children have always been symbols of innocence, goodness, and unlimited hope for the future,' Merlock Jackson writes. Prior to the Second World War, film portrayals of children were of unerring innocence, spawning popular child stars like Shirley Temple, Jackie Cooper and Judy Garland. Similar characterisations can be found in contemporary Steven Spielberg films like *E.T.*, and the box-office hit, *Home Alone*.

It would, however, be over-simplistic to assert that every child image on screen is so sugar sweet. Merlock Jackson notes that, starting in 1968 with Roman Polanski's *Rosemary's Baby*, a distinctly darker image of childhood began to emerge. In the 1970s with films like *The Exorcist*, and *The Omen* and in the 1980s with films like *Children of the Corn*, children possessed by evil spirits wreaked all sorts of havoc. She relates this to a new unease with parenthood due to soaring unemployment and a higher cost of living which meant that children were a huge financial burden; fears about overpopulation;

12

increase in divorce; and questions being raised about motherhood by the feminist movement.

Glorified parenthood and babies were again firmly on the agenda when, in the late 1980s, a rash of cradle comedies captured the public imagination. The first was *Raising Arizona,* which in the words of one critic, 'took a shrewd look at the way that people who've never really grown up themselves insist on their absolute right to parenthood'.[7] *Maybe Baby, Three Men and a Baby* and *Baby Boom* followed. The last of these especially captures anxieties felt about women who opt for careers rather than motherhood. In an article in *Film Comment* magazine, critic Marcia Pally describes it thus:

> To save herself from the sorrow of spinsterhood, she [Diane Keaton] chucks her business suit and million-dollar-a-year job for a house in Vermont, a real man (Sam Shepard), a baby, and spooning applesauce into little jars. Yech. Oh yes. She does turn the applesauce to profit in a cottage industry – but only to reject more firmly Big Bad Career.[8]

Advertisements also use idealised family situations to sell all manner of products. A picture is created of easy prosperity, marital harmony and appealing children. There are indirect messages that parenthood brings with it loving respect from children and when problems are presented, like the harassed mother in Oxo advertisements, there's total lack of gravity. Often the product is portrayed as an easy cure for the family malaise (see how they are united by their Oxo gravy). Children are sentimentalised in advertisements and used to sell products which have little or nothing to do with childhood, such as cars, building societies, soap powder and toilet rolls.

13

I asked my interviewees to comment on how the media portrays families and motherhood:

> Babies are seen as 'designer accessories', something to have after the car, house, etc. Nothing is ever said about how hard it is and that children are for life. (June, 28)

> It's far too idealistic and makes people think that's how life should be: clean, neat with three peaceful children. (Beverley, 44)

> Families are always stereotyped into the cosy mums having a coffee morning while the kids play in the garden. (Linda, 34)

> It's still rare to see a realistic portrayal of family life on TV, although I think there has been some improvement over the past decade. Advertising is as simple-minded as ever. (Julia, 32)

> It's disgusting, especially in women's magazines. Whenever somebody famous is interviewed the question of whether they will have children is always asked. Women are led to believe this is their function in life. (Jane, 29)

> It's hard for women to reject this image when they're totally surrounded by it. (Jo, 39)

Images of non-mothers

What are the media images of women who do not want to or cannot have children? They seem to fall into two distinct categories: the sad spinster and the neurotic career bitch. The latter has become very popular recently:

14

Glenn Close in *Fatal Attraction* (1987) is a supreme example. The film hinted at the fact that the character played by Close, a successful career woman, is unable to have children. She strings along her married lover (Michael Douglas) with lies about being pregnant, and then in a fit of jealousy when he chooses to stay with his wife and child, causes havoc in his family life by boiling his son's pet rabbit before finally going off the rails in his bathroom with a carving knife. The cuckolded wife (and mother), although represented as less sexually exciting than Glenn Close, is seen as loving, nurturing and sensible and the home she creates a sanctuary for a harassed New York businessman to rest his head. For a more recent, and equally neurotic child-free woman, there's Rebecca de Mornay in *The Hand That Rocks the Cradle* (1992). 'In idealising motherhood, a tremendous amount of denial has to take place and this denial is projected on to the figure of the childfree woman. She makes us anxious. Go and see *The Hand That Rocks the Cradle* to see just how anxious,' writes columnist Suzanne Moore in the *Guardian*[9] in a piece disputing 'the myth of the maternal instinct'.

De Mornay plays a doctor's wife who miscarries when her husband commits suicide, following the disclosure that he has been sexually abusing the pregnant women in his care. De Mornay is told that she will no longer be able to have children, and seeking revenge she takes the position of nanny in the household of the woman who reported her husband's misdemeanour. She then tries to steal her employer's family, turning the young daughter against her mother, trying to seduce the father and even secretly breast-feeding the new baby. There's little sympathy for this woman who has been through the most

15

appalling tragedy: she is portrayed as sadistic, cold, scheming and ultimately capable of murder. This is the fate of the woman who cannot fulfil her biological destiny.

I asked my interviewees to think of a positive media image of a child-free woman. Revealingly, they did not come up with a single example.

> Childless women are given a terribly negative image: the spinster in the lonely apartment. (Jo, 39)

> I can't think of a single example, positive or negative. (Julia, 32)

> Negative images abound – the sad spinster, the hard-nosed, avaricious career woman. Even the wonderful Bet Gilroy in *Coronation Street* nurses a secret heartache, having given up her son for adoption. (Helen, 26)

> Childless women are always portrayed as hard-bitten career girls, and men-haters. (Linda, 34)

> I don't remember many. Most seem to be the high-flying unrealistic career women, who never rank lower than upper management. It's probably meant to be positive, but has the opposite effect on me. Some women may not wish to work and yet not want children either. (Jane, 29)

> Women who don't want children are shown as empty-headed bimbos only interested in hedonistic pursuits, or hard-driven but ultimately unfulfilled career women who regret their choice when it is almost too late. Young women in the soaps who say they want careers not children are soon taught how empty this way of life would be, usually by being involved

in a moving experience with a supposedly adorable child, and allowing their 'real' feelings to show through. (Janet, 29)

Psychoanalysis

The neurotic child-free woman stereotype probably owes a lot to psychoanalysis: Freud has been a formidable source of pro-birth thought. Psychoanalysis views parenthood as the natural culmination of 'normal' development to adulthood: the true definition of making it to psychological normality is to be a heterosexual woman who is a mother, or a heterosexual man who is a father. Freud asserted that women compensated for their penis envy by having a child, and that a woman who did not seek fulfilment in childbearing might become neurotic. Accordingly, a woman's ultimate source of satisfaction lay in motherhood, particularly a relationship with a son:

> The only thing that brings a mother undiluted satisfaction is her relation to a son: it is quite the most complete relationship between human beings, and the one that is the most free from ambivalence. The mother can transfer to her son all the ambition which she has had to suppress in herself, and she can hope to get from him the satisfaction of all that has remained to her of her masculinity complex.[10]

Much has subsequently been written about Freud's misogyny and lack of empirical research, yet his psychology has been absorbed into Western popular culture and became a dominant form of psychiatry after the Second World War.

Many of the women I interviewed have been made to

17

feel that there is something 'wrong' with them psychologically:

> When I turn up for Christmas, unmarried and without children, my mother always says 'Where did I go wrong? There's something very peculiar about you.' (Sue, 33)

> I have occasionally been told that I'm abnormal and unnatural, but I have never let it bother me too much. I once had a letter published in a woman's magazine about the child-free choice, and was both amazed and surprised at the number of angry replies that were published the following week. Women wrote in extolling the joys of motherhood, and accusing me of just about everything, from being a child-hating lesbian to causing the decline of family values. The implication throughout them all was that I was somehow lacking as a woman, and that all normal, healthy people should be protected from people like me. (Janet, 29)

> Let's face it, being happily married for twelve years and not having children by choice is not normal. I worry that it is also unnatural and that there is something lacking in me. (Charlotte, 34)

> I once worked with a middle-aged man who thought that all unmarried/child-free women were 'peculiar'. (Julia, 32)

> Male friends at work try to wind me up by telling me that it's unnatural for a woman not to have children. People tend to think my husband and I are a bit way out because we don't have children, and have a house full of animals, including a tarantula spider.

They expect us to be weird. I had a woman from the *Telegraph* on the phone who was writing a piece about the child-free. She said, 'You sound so *normal*. I don't mean that to be an insult.' Does she expect a two-headed monster? (Jane, 29)

I was always odd and considered eccentric because I couldn't conform to what was expected of me. (Maud, 75)

Years ago my father-in-law was quite adamant I'd have children and I'd love them. Now his son has had the op [vasectomy] he acts as if I cast an evil spell over him. (Linda, 34)

Casual remarks

'Just you wait till you have children . . .' is a familiar litany that reinforces the inevitability of parenthood. 'Have you got children?' is a polite question asked at social gatherings. When couples marry, pressure is soon put upon them to start reproducing. 'It'll be your turn next,' says someone to the young couple, when another family member or friend has a baby. I recently heard someone describe a young married child-free man as 'putting in practice' when he bathed his little nephew. Such seemingly superficial remarks are commonplace for the women I interviewed:

I can remember my mother-in-law making one or two remarks about how she wanted grandchildren, and how couples who didn't have children were selfish. I didn't even answer her. (Josephine, 63)

19

My parents have never pressured me to have children, but I know they would like to have grandchildren one day, and they make joking comments about it now and then. My husband comes from a very traditional child-centred family: we have felt pressure from them and I think it will increase with time. His mother doesn't take me seriously; she thinks I don't know my own mind and that I'll feel differently once the biological clock starts ticking. She always talks about 'when' rather than 'if' we have children, regardless of what I say. My husband's three sisters have seven children between them, and the kids are always the main focus of conversation when we're together. I often feel excluded in their company, especially as they're often laughing and saying things like, 'You'll learn, once you have your own.' (Janet, 29)

My parents always ask me when I'm going to 'settle down'. I hate that term, it makes me cringe. I still don't know what it's supposed to mean. (Marnie, 31)

A long time ago my mother said it was 'selfish' of me not to want children. (Coral, 43)

My parents always spend Christmas with my brothers rather than us, because they say 'Christmas is for children.' (Georgina, 32)

My husband's parents don't know that we don't want children, and keep using the phrase, 'they haven't got children *yet*'. (Bethany, 22)

Recently my mother-in-law made comments to the effect that others in the family who are bringing up children are doing a worthwhile job: in other words, my life and career are dismissed as unimportant. (Patricia, 34)

Sometimes the same message can be conveyed without words. Elizabeth, 26, notices that her mother deliberately makes an exaggerated fuss of children in her presence, the unspoken undercurrent being, 'Why don't we have any grandchildren yet? Look how happy it would make me? Don't you feel guilty?'

Women who are married are under much more pressure than those who are single or cohabiting. Says Jane, who's been married for four years: 'No one talked to me about children until after I had got married. Previously I had lived with a boyfriend for four years, but my mother had never mentioned the subject.' As can be seen from some of the examples above, particular pressure comes from mothers-in-law who feel it's the wife's duty to provide her son with a child, and that somehow he is being denied his right as a man.

Direct pressure

Casual barbed comments about not having children were reported as commonplace. Women are frequently subjected to more direct pressure to 'settle down' and start a family. This often comes from would-be grandparents:

I haven't told my dad I don't want children because it would hurt him too much. The part of me that does want children is partly for him: he's getting on, and it would be a sad thing for him to die and not see me a mother. He wants to see his children settled, and by that he means, married with children. If I reach 30 and still haven't got space in my life for children, I imagine they will all get pretty concerned. (Emily, 22)

I get less pressure from my parents now, they've mellowed out a bit. They used to say things like, 'I don't know what's the matter with you. Your boyfriends never come to anything, and we've given up hope that we'll have grandchildren.' I'd say, 'Well, dream on, mother. Why can't you go and work with the Brownies again like you used to – there are enough kids there.' (Sue, 33)

My mother-in-law and father-in-law pressurise me. My father-in-law went so far as to say he thought there was something wrong with people who didn't like children. My mother-in-law goes really stupid over babies and really cannot understand anyone not being tolerant of children's ways. I just feel she doesn't accept my decision and that I'm depriving her son. (Debbie, 34)

My sister has no qualifications and has never worked. She lives with a violent boyfriend and his dad and brother, and slaves for them all. But at 24 she has three children, this makes her a real woman: my mum and dad feel my sister has succeeded where I have failed and I know they don't understand and tease me. (Helen, 26)

Tanujah, a youth worker, says that in the Asian community it is extremely unusual for a woman to choose not to have children. As yet she hasn't dared mention the subject to her family. 'I don't know how it will affect me. Because I'm not married it isn't too bad at the moment. It's a real blow for Asian women who can't have children: they're not considered real women.'

The pressure put on women often fades with time. Morag, a 37-year-old finance manager who was sterilised at 24 says: 'My husband's family used to comment, but have given up after almost twenty years.' A few women seem to have escaped intense family pressure. 'No one has ever mentioned it,' says Margaret, 48, a secretary who has been married for seventeen years. 'They seem to have accepted how I am, although occasionally I'll see mum gazing wistfully at neighbours' grandchildren or hear her speak slightly enviously about someone whose daughter has produced a grandchild,' says Linda, 34, a housewife, who has been married eighteen months. 'My parents have never mentioned it at all,' says Jo, 39, who works as a teacher and has been with her partner for fifteen years. 'I am extremely lucky in so far as my parents supported my decision. I was about 12 when I told my mother that I never wanted to get married or have children and she never tried to change my mind,' says 32-year-old Julia who works as a core dresser in a foundry. Says Annabelle, a 49-year-old musician, 'My in-laws were wonderful and said, "Don't feel you've got to provide any more grandchildren – the six we already have is more than enough".'

Feeling alone

According to estimates from the Office of Population Censuses and Surveys, around 12 per cent of women haven't had children by the age of 45. Figures in America and Canada estimate that 5–7 per cent of couples don't have children through choice. Children are the passport to a 'normal' mainstream lifestyle. Many interviewees claimed that not having children means not being able to join in.

Numerous social activities are organised around children, especially when they are young. Conversation is child-centred: has the baby learnt to walk yet? What school will your little girl be going to ? Isn't he getting a big boy? Cars and houses are designed with the average family of four in mind. The fabric of our life is family based: family entertainment, family holidays, family-sized packaging at the supermarket, family festivities like Christmas and Easter. It's hardly surprising that women who choose not to have children say they feel marginalised, and sometimes isolated and excluded.

Maud, 75, worked as a nurse in London before she retired to Devon. Although her mother and sister supported her decision not to have children, she says she feels especially isolated because a class barrier has confounded the problem: 'Other women who decided not to have children were not in my class. I'm sorry to use that word, but it does come down to that. They would have been upper middle-class women, well educated, and I was working class. I met them in London through my nursing: I remember one woman psychologist. But they were not the women with whom my income allowed me to live.'

> I spend a lot of time feeling that I *ought* to have children and feel very lonely and left out because that's what my generation and peers are doing. I don't meet many people in a similar position to me and I find it hard to make friends. It's bloody hard to meet up with other women who will admit to feeling this way, never mind about starting up friendships. Most people seem to assume you want children and can't have them. (Debbie, 34)

24

> Often in a social situation I feel the odd one out. As far as my Jewish community is concerned I'm a complete write-off: you're a woman, you don't marry and you don't have children as well. That means I'm a non-person. (Marion, 41)

The women frequently complained that friends would drift away when they became parents. Having a baby changes a person's life immeasurably: babies are time-consuming, demanding and alter the focus and pattern of one's existence. We tend to mix with people with whom we have something in common, and mothers find tremendous support in having relationships with other mothers. They can share concerns, offer each other advice and divide the school runs. Mothers might find that they have precious little time for socialising, and therefore have to be especially selective about who they choose to have friendships with. Often it's the child-free women who are dropped from the social calendar. This can be a source of anger and hurt. Says Janet, 29: 'When a new baby arrives all of a sudden it seems that the rest of the world can go to hell, all that matters is what's best for baby. To me it seems that they've deliberately chosen to live in a narrow restricted world, with the petty concerns of their own little corner of it being the only things they really care about. They obviously feel that I can in no way understand the momentous thing that's happened to them. We each feel let down by the other, with nothing left in common. I think it's a pity this has to happen, but I really don't see a way around it.' Debbie, a 34-year-old clerical assistant, is similarly upset: 'I have lost all my friends over the past ten years as they have all had children. This seems to make it impossible for them to socialise.'

It works both ways: the child-free woman also withdraws from friends who become parents. She might find herself bored with the baby-orientated conversation, or discover that her nerves get quickly frayed by the noisy demands of her friends' children. 'I've grown away from my friends with children,' says Marion, 41. 'Lorraine, my closest girl-friend, got married at 19 to an Italian and had children, and kept on having children. I was interested in Lorraine having children because she was my closest friend, but apart from that it didn't interest me. I lost interest in my other friends: the domestic situation bored me. I suppose I made other friends through sharing flats and work: I moved on.'

One woman, Coral, a 43-year-old academic book editor, chose to move away when her flatmate became pregnant: 'She decided to have a baby, as she was 35 and getting on a bit. She didn't tell me at first because she knew I'd think this was a bummer of an idea. I knew she'd expect me and the other flatmates to act as surrogate parents. I didn't particularly want to share a house with a baby in it. It wasn't my idea of heaven, thank you very much. So I left, and she was not pleased with me. My women friends don't really have children. When one's friends have children it's a point of reference you don't have with them. For them it's the all-consuming part of their life but I'm just not terribly interested in children, and not remotely interested in having conversations about children: babies in nappies, schools, washing machines. I'm terminally bored.'

Mothers vs. non-mothers

While writing this book I noticed many mothers bristle at mention of the subject matter: faces have dropped

26

instantly, hackles are raised. This is very difficult terrain. We are acutely aware that to become a mother means becoming a second-class citizen: mothers aren't paid; they aren't seen to be professional or trained for anything; they are immobile because our built environment is so hostile to children; worst of all their intellectual status is equated with the children they are raising. How then can we begin to talk about being child-free without mothers, who are already sensitive to criticism, feeling that this amounts to innate disapproval of their role? Judith D. Schwartz's book *The Mother Puzzle* sums up the dilemma:

> How can we celebrate women's 'difference' without allowing the ideology of difference to subordinate us and negate our rights (as has happened in the past)? How can we affirm the significance of motherhood while still trying to free women from the obligation to mother?[11]

Amelia, a 22-year-old civil servant, feels that her decision to remain child-free is interpreted as disapproval of her friends who have children. 'Many of my friends in their late twenties and early thirties are beginning to have children,' she says. 'I feel reluctant to see them because I'll have to be polite about their children and apologetic that my decision isn't related to them and their children.'

Sadly, these tensions between women mean that sometimes it is easier for mothers and child-free women not to continue or initiate friendships. Ruth, a 56-year-old engineer, finds relationships with other child-free women more satisfying, and deliberately seeks them out: 'Most of my friends are people who don't have children. I don't think my relationships with people who have children are as close as people without, as emotionally children are a strong tie for them. Also physically it's harder to arrange to do things. After my husband died I made a conscious effort to make new friends: I met two child-free friends on a walking holiday and skiing holiday.'

One woman, Charlotte, a 34-year-old librarian, felt rather betrayed by a close friend who planned to have a baby without telling her. 'We used to do a great deal together and see each other a lot, but she didn't give me a hint she was planning to start a family. It was very hurtful when I found out, and altered the basis of the relationship. It was bound to make a difference, however amicably we agree to disagree. This friend and I cannot see why each has made the decision she has.'

No babies, no problem

Happily, not all friendships break down with the advent of parenthood. Some women, realising the possible differences that might arise when friends have babies, make a great effort to sustain their close relationship.

> My closest friend is about to have a baby, and I will make a big effort to keep in close contact. She knows exactly how I feel about children, but I will make an effort to be approving and friendly. I've already said I don't think I'll be very good at babysitting. I've told her stories about children I've babysat for and dreadful things happening: pushing them on the swing until they were sick because I had no idea. I'll be disappointed if she turns into the sort of person who cannot have a serious conversation with you while the kid is in the room because all she can do is make gooey baby noises. (Sue, 33)

I can think of one friend in particular who has fitted her new daughter into her life with a minimum of fuss; while obviously her life has had to change, motherhood has not become her sole focus in life. She has kept up with her work and with other interests, her activities have not all become child-centred, and others are not expected to dote on her child, but just to treat her with politeness and respect. This friend and I are still very close. (Penny, 30)

Karen, a 36-year-old musician in a symphony orchestra, feels that the child-free issue has little impact on her friendships with women. 'Roughly half of my friends do have children, half don't,' she explains. 'As far as I'm concerned, people take me for what I am. Deciding to be child-free is just one aspect of me. How it affects the friendship depends on the individual or couple. They decide to be child-free for different reasons; some of those I empathise with, and some not. These friendships are no more or less important to me than with mothers.' Vicky, 37, agrees that the child status issue has little bearing on her relationships: 'A number of my friends have had children recently in their mid- to late thirties. I honestly don't think it's altered the basis of the relationship as my husband and I knew them for years before the children were born. I suppose there's a little less time to see them now.'

Needing other child-free friends

Few of us like to feel we are completely alone in our decision; in the words of one woman, 'It's nice to know other people feel the same way too.' Even though a small minority of women don't have children, somehow some of those for whom childlessness comes through choice manage to find each other and draw strength from the friendships. It was through this network of child-free friends that I found many of the women who agreed to be interviewed for this book.

> It's a great relief to be able to talk to other women who feel the same, who understand me and with whom I can discuss things like my intention to be sterilised. (Amelia, 22)

> My best friend has the same feelings as me and has also been sterilised. It's a real help to talk to someone who *really* understands how I feel. (Georgina, 32)

> Two of my closest friends are child-free, but are 5–8 years younger so may change their decision over time. We do spend a lot of time talking around the issue and it is important to feel you are not totally isolated in your decision. (Jo, 39)

> My relationships with child-free women are very important to me: they're my best friends. We are much more on the same wavelength as our lifestyles are similar. Altogether it is a much more relaxed type of relationship. (Patricia, 34)

'I don't know any other women who have chosen to remain child-free: I wish I did,' says 37-year-old Gail, an office temp from Essex. In 1978, in response to the isolation that some of the child-free experience, a small group of people who were then involved with the National Association of the Childless (now called ISSUE) formed a new group: the British Organisation of Non-Parents (BON). ISSUE is a national organisation which supports people with fertility problems: it provides information and puts the infertile in touch with each other. Its primary objective is to help those who want children but are having problems conceiving (about one in six couples). Root Cartwright, chairman of BON, says that the needs of those who choose not to have children weren't adequately dealt with within the structure of ISSUE. 'We became aware that the issue was not as straightforward as it seemed to be,' says Cartwright. 'The business of finding that you can't have children is complex, and in amongst all the people who were presenting the problems of grief and horror were people who didn't really want to have kids, so we decided to set something up that represented that point of view.'

BON, which is based in Edinburgh, has 150 members nationwide: not a high number for an organisation which has been established fifteen years. Cartwright explains that it has a high turnover of membership: 'There are two reasons for that. It's not the kind of thing that lends itself to activities. You can't really sit around in a village hall once a week not having children. In earlier years we tried to have a social aspect but nothing really happened.' He also points out that membership tends to be short-lived. 'They get involved when it's a hot issue for them; while they're in the throes of the decision-making process, or while they're being given a hard time by their family and friends. They derive the support and solidarity that they need on a short-term basis, and then they can't be bothered to renew their membership.'

BON provides members with a yearly newsletter, and the opportunity to meet other child-free people at a summer AGM in London. The organisation hopes to raise the profile of the child-free and has a positive attitude towards press enquiries. If you see a child-free

31

couple interviewed on television or in the press, the chances are they have been found through BON. About half of my case histories are BON members. 'We just want to make the thing public and say, "Hey look, there's a lot of people who feel this way. We're not Martians or criminals, or lunatics: we just don't want children," ' says Cartwright, who was sterilised when he was 33.

The majority of BON members are women and men in their mid-twenties to early forties: two-thirds are in couples, and one-third is single. Many discover the organisation through magazine and newspaper features. It survives financially purely on membership and doesn't have the budget to advertise.

The members I interviewed expressed relief that they had found BON, and gratitude for the support it offers:

> My husband and I joined BON for a feeling of solidarity. We also wanted to broaden our ideas and be aware of wider issues. (Vicky, 37)

> I needed someone to tell me I wasn't alone in feeling as I did. Also I had very nearly given in to a 'broody' phase encouraged by my mother-in-law. I felt I had almost given in to the pressure and needed someone to tell me I was right after all. (Debbie, 34)

> I joined when my last main ally, or so I thought, became pregnant. I was very depressed, lying awake at night, and needed some reassurance that I wasn't seriously abnormal. (Charlotte, 34)

The search for a sanctuary

Few of us want to be outsiders: we like to belong to a group of people; to be accepted and to share a rhythm of life

YOU *WILL* BE MOTHER

with our peers. Some of the child-free women identified themselves as having found a sub-culture or, in the words of 75-year-old Maud, 'a world within a world' where they felt at home. For Maud it came through her nursing career:

'Nursing was like a refuge. The medical profession is a world within a world, like the legal profession. Within it I didn't feel odd. In nursing you're not asked whether you've got children, and if it did come up they were only too glad you didn't, because it meant I could work all the weekends and Bank Holidays that others didn't want to work. In fact I used to get rather annoyed about it, because they'd say "Well, you haven't got any children." and I'd say, "But I do have a private life." '

Lucy, 69, a retired civil servant, makes a similar comment about her workplace: 'I didn't feel different by not having children, but by not having got married, because it was a bit of a disgrace to be a spinster. We don't use that term so much now. There were a lot of spinsters in the civil service, it wasn't so unusual there.'

Similarly, Karen works as a professional musician in a symphony orchestra. She and her husband agree that they don't want children. She says she does not feel unusual in her decision as the orchestra is a unique environment, and she knows of ten other female colleagues who choose to be child-free. 'I think of the people I work with who have children and it's a juggling act. We have a mother of one young child who came back to work after six months. Her husband is also in the orchestra so they have a dual problem because they're working the same schedules. Their son has had three live-in nannies, and every week they have to sit down and draw up a timetable of when they need their nanny day to day. I mean, really, I wish I could say the mother was a happy woman. There has been talk in the past of a crèche attached to the orchestra, but who's going to look after little ones until 12.30 at night?' Karen says that because so many of her colleagues have also chosen not to have children 'I don't feel odd, and I think my decision is respected. Whether they "understand" is another matter, but then I don't understand what drives people to want to become parents with all the attendant hassles that that status brings.'

Josephine, a 63-year-old retired teacher, says with amusement that she thinks of her friends as 'refugees'. Josephine is separated from her Italian husband, yet they live in different flats within the same house. 'My friends are a bit like me,' she says. 'A lot of them have got estrangements from their families and difficult family backgrounds, odd relationships. Perhaps refugees recognise each other: I can't think of a single close friend who has got a so-called normal happy family life.' Josephine lives in London and believes that the capital is especially welcoming to people who live outside the conventions. 'It's easier here. I've always been aware that London is a refuge for refugees because you're so free, nobody is too concerned because London is impersonal. Nobody expects anything of you: you're just there.'

Dianne at 28 is a younger child-free woman who identifies herself as belonging to a sub-culture of like-minded people. She is bisexual and mixes with many gay people. 'I'm lucky in that I have a lot of single friends and gay male friends who haven't got children. I don't feel like I'm surrounded by married women having children.' She works as a press officer for a charity and believes that the voluntary sector attracts women who have slightly unconventional attitudes and lifestyles.

34

Marion, 41, works as a journalist, which she too sees as an atypical working environment. She believes she was attracted to this career because it broke away dramatically from her orthodox Jewish upbringing. 'I was always attracted to unconventional environments,' she says. 'Anywhere there were a lot of people to meet. I found that in the media. It's also a male-dominated environment, and an easy way to meet men. In a way I was trying to get as far as possible away from my Jewish background which was very family based. We lived in Stamford Hill where there were lots of Jewish people, and I went to a Jewish school. It was an environment where girls got engaged at 17, and were married by 20. It was expected that was what I would do, but I couldn't see myself married. In the Jewish environment everything focuses on the family: weddings, engagements, bar mitzvahs. The family is the focus of family life and I was often coerced to go to family dos when I was younger. I didn't like them. To me the concept of family was like obligation. My father always used to say we were going to "pay our respects" to our grandparents: it wasn't something you did spontaneously because you loved being with these people. As an only child I was quite stifled; my parents were well meaning but over-protective. To me the idea of family was something I wanted to get away from.'

Marion left her family thousands of miles away when, in her early thirties, she went to live in Sydney, Australia, where she found a peer group she describes as 'fairly unconventional, only a few had kids'. However, she found Sydney less accommodating to the child-free than London: 'In Australia I always had to justify myself and I got sick to death with it. In London I don't find it a problem: there are so many different races and creeds.

Everybody blends in. In London everybody is that bit different.' By comparison, Katy, 23, who comes from a village in Somerset, says, 'It's so much the done thing to have children here that it really stands out when people don't. I can tell that people think I'm abnormal.'

Free to choose?

The feminist movement has espoused the idea of choice: I should be free to have an abortion, should I choose; I should be free to work and be a mother, should I choose. In this book, freedom of choice is about not having children, but how free are we *really* to make this decision? For true free choice we need to stand apart from coercion and assimilate what is right for us as individuals. Having children is a precious and huge responsibility that is not right for everyone: nor is everyone right for it. Ideally parenthood should be something we consciously choose to do, not an event that steamrollers our lives when we are looking the other way. How many people become parents because they cannot see what else life offers them? Because they assume that's what one ought to do? Of course we must also acknowledge that not absolutely everything is within our control: some women are physically unable to have children; others have unplanned pregnancies.

We need to question what has always been unquestionable: why does my role as a woman necessarily involve motherhood? Being pressurised into having children is about conformity; it ensures that society is manageable, and in particular has served to keep women in the home and out of public life. Being able to discern this pressure is the first step towards true free choice about becoming, or not becoming, a mother.

2

PREGNANCY AND THE
MATERNAL INSTINCT

PREGNANCY and childbirth are major experiences in a
woman's life. Even women who are definite in their
decision not to have children have contemplated what
childbearing must be like. Unsurprisingly, the women I
spoke to expressed many anxieties and fears about pain
and discomfort, even death. Some enjoyed imagining the
birth process, and expressed regrets that they might never
know childbearing in its magnitude. No one said that she
didn't want children solely because of her anxieties about
childbearing; this was just one of many reasons in the
whole tapestry of motivations. In the words of one
woman, 'It supports and confirms my decision.'

It is only since 1956 and the founding of the Natural
Childbirth Association (now called the National Childbirth Trust) that childbirth has come to be viewed as a
positive experience for women. Sheila Kitzinger, famed
voice of the movement, wrote lyrically of the moment of

delivery: 'The woman begins to feel herself gradually opening up, like a bud into full flower.' For the first time childbirth took root in the imagination as something that might actually be pleasurable, a markedly different approach to the biblical decree that 'In sorrow thou shalt bring forth children.' 'For the conscious woman who is participating actively in labour, the moment when the head crowns is an intensely pleasurable and very exciting one,' writes Kitzinger.[1] Until as little as a hundred years ago childbirth was a major killer of women, second only to tuberculosis for women of childbearing age. Before 1800 up to 1.5 per cent of all births ended in the mother's death. A typical woman had six children, which meant that her risk of dying in childbirth increased to around 9 per cent. Medical advances in the 1870s started a downward trend in maternal mortality, but before that childbirth really could be extremely grim. A woman might be left to die in agony when there were problems in childbirth, simply because the midwives and doctors did not know what could be done. Before 1900 the average woman was likely to spend five hours longer in labour than she is today. Some of the worst horror stories include women haemorrhaging because midwives believed the placenta should be forcibly ripped out of the uterus immediately after the baby was born; when the baby was stuck they would try to pull it out by grabbing whatever was available, sometimes tearing the child. In his book *A History of Women's Bodies*,[2] Edward Shorter reports that one midwife accidentally decapitated a child. He also reports that in Britain before 1858, a Caesarean was like a death sentence; of 80 performed only 29 per cent of women survived, others dying either from infection or the shock of the pain.

Pain relief was unavailable to poor women up until the beginning of this century. Most deliveries happened at home and a common practice was to tie a towel around the bedstead for the delivering woman to grip when the pain became overwhelming.

Stories of maternal deaths or difficult births would have circulated faster than a bush fire, instilling fear and dread in women approaching pregnancy, especially for the first time. Even today, when the risks of mortality have been almost completely eradicated (there were only 45 maternal deaths in 1991 out of 699,200 births) and painkilling drugs are commonplace, women still talk openly with each other about how excruciating childbirth can be. The words of a conversation I heard still echo alarmingly in my ear: 'Nothing had prepared me for the pain. If there had been a gun beside the bed I would have shot myself.'

Literature, film and television often reinforce the agonies of childbirth. In soap opera a problematic delivery bolsters the ratings. When one is brought up hearing such macabre stories, pregnancy for the first time is a fearful prospect. Primarily it is a fear of the unknown: how bad is the pain exactly? Will the baby tear me to shreds? For some women childbirth is something they feel they have no control over; an event that happens to them rather than something in which they participate. The ultimate question has to be: will I die? Feminists have suggested that this question incorporates more than just death in the physical sense. In 1976 when Adrienne Rich published *Of Woman Born*[3] she proposed that giving birth might also involve the death of a woman's life as it was:

Typically, under patriarchy, the mother's life is exchanged for the child; her autonomy as a separate being seems fated to conflict with the infant she will bear. The self-denying, self-annihilative role of the Good Mother (linked implicitly with suffering and with the repression of anger) will spell the 'death' of the woman or girl who once had hopes, expectations, fantasies *for herself* – especially when those hopes and fantasies have never been acted upon.

The same idea was put forward twenty-seven years earlier when Simone de Beauvoir quoted Hegel in *The Second Sex*:

> Caught up in the great cycle of the species, she affirms life in the teeth of time and death; in this she glimpses immortality; but in her flesh she feels the truth of Hegel's words: 'The birth of children is the death of parents.' The child, he says, again, is 'the very being of their love which is external to them', and inversely the child will attain his own being 'in separating from its source, a separation in which that source finds its end'.[4]

Pregnancy repulsion

The most frequent responses to my question; 'How does the thought of childbirth make you feel?' were 'Yuk!' and 'Sick!': one-word exclamations that forcefully express abhorrence. When questioned further, some of the women were profoundly disturbed by the thought or spectacle of childbirth; even to the point of fainting, as in the case of one nurse who, one would assume, might be less inclined towards squeamishness. 'Childbirth makes me want to cross my legs and I feel sick,' says Georgina, 32. 'It was the only thing that caused me to pass out during my nurse training.'

Julia, 32, similarly says that she finds childbirth more difficult to contemplate than any surgical process; 'It makes me feel sick. I can quite happily watch all sorts of surgical operations on TV, but childbirth in close-up living colour has me reaching for the off switch. Give me a nice appendectomy any day. Similarly, whenever the conversation veers towards labour pains, stitches and stretch marks I can usually be seen heading for the door'.

Emily, 22, also says that seeing childbirth on television made her nauseous. 'I'm totally squeamish,' she exclaims. 'The very first time I saw a birth on television I was sick, but I was fascinated. It's horrifying. I can't imagine what the pain is like, and I have a total fear of everything that could go wrong.'

On breaking down the numerous responses I had from women who felt repulsion at the thought of childbirth and pregnancy, I identified several different reactions. Most universal was the fear of pain during childbirth, and also the discomfort of pregnancy. Says 29-year-old Janet: 'I think pregnancy would be hideous. Pregnant women look so ungainly and uncomfortable to me, I can't imagine it being an enjoyable experience. What possible reason would I have for wanting to carry a heavy, kicking load in front of me for months on end, unable to put it down for a minute even to sleep? I've had back trouble all my life, and can just imagine how pregnancy would aggravate it!'

'I'm glad I'll never experience such pain: all I have heard from pregnant friends is about the appalling sick feeling, the backaches, the indigestion, the sleepless nights, the feeling of being enormous. This could only appeal to a masochist,' says 34-year-old Louise. Lurid stories of difficult labours and uncomfortable pregnancies were especially fresh in the minds of the women whose contemporaries were currently having children. For one woman it was her mother who first planted the seeds of anxiety. 'My mother used the fear of childbirth as if it were a contraceptive,' remembers 69-year-old Lucy. 'That's how it came over to me. I can remember her words, "Men only want a woman for one thing", and she described childbirth as the most awful pain in the world. She certainly rang warning bells for me, and it struck horror in me.' Before Lucy was born, her mother had had a backstreet abortion, a story which further reinforced Lucy's abhorrence of anything to do with childbirth. 'I wondered how she could have gone through with it. There were no anaesthetics or anything. She told me they'd cut the womb with a razor, which started contractions. How can somebody hold still whilst that's happening? The whole thing appeared horrible to me and I didn't want any part of it. I was very frightened of the physical side of it. I didn't so much think I would die, from the novels I used to read so many women did die in childbirth, but I feared a long painful labour.'

Angie, 27, a theatre spotlight operator, also picked up a lot of fear about childbirth from her mother. When Angie was in her late teens, her mother had another child. 'Came the actual night when she was ready to give birth I went with her in the ambulance,' remembers Angie. 'It was just so painful to see mum going through labour pains. It was awkward for both of us. I didn't known whether to stay and comfort her, or what. Her labour pains lasted about fourteen hours. Seeing her there, it was awful. It put me off. I could have been there when she gave birth, but felt really embarrassed about it so didn't. I saw her afterwards and there was this wrinkled bloody little thing. Odd. It frightened me.'

Being in pain is a lonely place. A woman in labour may be surrounded by people in the delivery room, yet only she can give birth. There's no reason at all to suppose that women who don't want children have lower pain thresholds than women who want to become mothers. Nor is there reason to believe that women who do want to become mothers fear childbirth any less. But what is often said about childbirth is that it is the pain that is the soonest forgotten, because of the overwhelming joy of being presented with an infant one has longed for. For women who don't want children there is no light at the end of the tunnel when contemplating the agonies of childbirth. The baby is purely secondary, an after-thought. 'I'm revolted and appalled that medical science hasn't come up with solutions to make all the horrors and after-effects easier. All that agony and at the end of it you've only got a baby,' says 22-year-old Amelia dismissively.

Another fear centred on the idea of something alien growing within the woman's body. A developing child was not contemplated as a life that was a benign extension of the mother, but as a hostile intrusion that would sap her energies. Pregnancy was viewed as an invasion of her inner world. Words used to describe the foetus or baby were typically 'it', 'this thing', even 'parasite'. A psychotherapist spoke of one of her clients describing the foetus very unpleasantly as the 'little cancer within'. 'The idea of something growing inside me scares me,' says 29-year-old Maria. Siobhan, 30, is aware that her feelings set her apart from other women she knows. 'It doesn't appeal to me at all, the idea of something growing in my stomach. To a lot of other women it means being able to create something that is your own, that's yours. It must be a very powerful feeling, but I don't feel it at all. I don't know why I'm different.' Many women who'd had abortions described their feelings about early pregnancy in this way.

What seems to be common to all these reactions is the fear of losing control; of surrendering the autonomy which they have achieved. Independence and self-determination are qualities that have been exalted in the past decades of the feminist movement, and the women pride themselves on having won them. For women child-birth means entering the realm of the psyche that is at the mercy of the unpredictable force of nature. No matter how much control a woman tries to gain over childbirth through pre-natal classes and preparatory reading, there is still that part of the birth process that is beyond reach. It means becoming vulnerable, even helpless. This vulnerability is both feared and despised. Marnie, 31, bitterly describes how she witnessed this at first hand when she worked as an auxiliary nurse at Guy's Hospital, in London, in the labour and maternity ward. 'I watched all these babies being born: it was dreadful, awful. Everyone was there like fat cows lolling in their beds doing what they were told. There was only one positive birth I saw: it was actually my friend. She turned up saying she felt labour pains, and they said, "Go away it won't be for ages." I said, "Please have it today so that I can be there." And she was right. She came back later that day. She was 28 and it was her second child. She gave birth on the floor on her knees. She was the only one I saw who did anything different.

'I don't think I'm afraid of giving birth, it's more the worry afterwards. I just remember these women lying with their legs in stirrups being stitched up. It was such a bloody mess: there's not a single part left of you that you can recognise. It's like something from the butcher's shop. You can have drugs and things, but that makes you even more helpless. If you have an epidural the baby has to be dragged out.'

Some women also expressed anxieties about losing their sexual appeal. Pregnancy was equated with obesity. 'I'm too concerned about my figure,' says 34-year-old Linda. 'I would hate putting on all that weight and I enjoy being fit and slim,' says 42-year-old Rose, who is a keen runner and goes on marathons with her husband. Women valued the power their sex appeal gave them over men, and feared a loss in status if that were to be taken away. Says Miriam, 33: 'My husband thinks pregnant women look grotesque and so do I. I can't imagine how anyone could fancy a bloated blob.'

Miriam is picking up on a common male anxiety about the connection between maternity and sex. Obviously the two are intimately entwined, yet men strain to keep them separated. Women's breasts are glorified daily in national newspapers as playthings for men, yet breastfeeding in restaurants and public places is frowned upon or forbidden. It is not unusual for men to have affairs while their partners are pregnant, and at worst I've heard of philandering husbands being with their lovers instead of at the birth of their child. Women are not immune to these male feelings: they pick them up, and take on the confusion. A pregnancy is hard to ignore, and that swelling bump shouts out a message loud and clear: this woman has had sexual intercourse. Pregnancy exposes women as women, and for those who did not like their bodies prior to these dramatic changes, it furthers dislike, and increases feelings of vulnerability. For other women, pregnancy can be very attractive. 'It's a very feminine thought being pregnant: the big tummy and swelling breasts,' marvels 22-year-old Emily.

Pregnancy interest

Often these stories of traumatic childbirth experiences were told with relish: as well as being repelled, the women were also compelled by them, rather like the cathartic pleasures of watching a horror film. 'I'm terrified at the thought of childbirth but also interested,' explains 39-year-old Jo.

One woman's fascination with childbirth led her to vicariously experience it herself. Lucy, now 69, had a pregnancy scare in her younger years, and made a pact with God that if it turned out to be a false alarm she would help another woman who was pregnant. She rejoiced when her period eventually started, and true to her word joined the Natural Childbirth Trust, because 'I was anxious to see what could be done to improve childbirth for women: I wanted to know all that I could.' Later when returning from an out-of-town conference, Lucy befriended a pregnant woman on a train. The woman was single, and Lucy told her about the Natural Childbirth Trust, suggesting she accompany her to antenatal classes. 'I think she appreciated it,' remembers Lucy. 'The birth went well and although the hospital told her to be quiet she went on yelling and puffing.' When Lucy heard news of her friend's safe delivery she felt overjoyed.

Many of the women I interviewed expressed some sadness and regret that they would never experience the drama of childbirth. 'From what I've heard it's a unique experience and obviously very satisfying. Even if I don't want to do it it would be interesting to know what it's like,' says 56-year-old Ruth. Coral, 42, echoes Ruth's curiosity: 'I have wondered about what it would be like. One friend of mine said that she really liked being pregnant. She really liked the physical experience of being pregnant, and I thought this was the most extraordinary thing I'd ever heard in my life. I thought: aren't people wonderful? Such vastly different views. It did make me wonder if I would like it. In an intellectual fashion I'd quite like to know what it's like to be pregnant and have a baby, but I wouldn't like it emotionally enough to go off and do it.' Another woman identified her feelings about childbearing with those of men. 'I'm mildly curious as to how I would handle it, but only in the way a man might wonder, knowing it could never possibly happen to him,' says Linda, 34. 'I'm astonished that anyone could put themselves through something so painful and undignified, conceding that for a loving couple who truly want a baby it must be a wonderful sharing experience.'

'I'd love to experience it just to know what it feels like,' said Janette, a 30-year-old woman who recently had an abortion when she and her husband decided that they would be happier remaining child-free. 'When I was pregnant it was pretty awful as I felt so ill at the time, but I'd like to know what the latter stages feel like. I wonder if I could handle childbirth, what my pain threshold would be and how strong I'd be at the time.'

Helen, 26, works as a medical support worker on a gynaecology ward, an experience which she believes has made her examine more deeply her feelings about the birth process. Each day she works with patients admitted for a termination. Having always been strongly pro-choice in the abortion debate, Helen recently asked for a temporary transfer to the labour ward. 'Abortion isn't a black and white issue,' she explains. 'There's this new medical abortion drug and we do all the pilots for Sheffield. It's so easy that some women are starting to use it as their form of contraception. I've had to really start thinking about how I feel about this, and abortion on demand. I've witnessed late terminations, where they cut the baby up. A baby looks like a baby quite early on in a pregnancy, and it gets quite big fairly early on as well. I've seen a termination at 15 weeks and that was quite nasty. It has made it more real for me. If I were to get pregnant now I would have a termination, but I can see that it is a potential human being.' Helen, a Catholic who occasionally attends mass, asked for her transfer because 'I found that working with terminations day in and day out was starting to get on top of me. Maybe it's me being a Catholic. I was just seeing the negative side, death. I went to the labour ward because I thought it was important to see life.' Firm in her decision that she doesn't want children, Helen was surprised at how emotional she felt when watching her first delivery. 'When the baby cried, I cried. It's just a miracle and definitely moved me. I felt sad that I wouldn't ever experience it. What must it be like? To actually hold it for the first time, to think I'll never know that.' Conversely she also felt a relief that she would be spared the physical hardship: 'Nine months carting it around and then the labour. It's really painful and messy. I certainly couldn't see any of the joy of labour that you hear about. That's just a load of crap where I was standing.'

Bethany, 22, said she would definitely consider surrogacy for money, such was her interest in birth. Ilona,

43, an ex-midwife, has also contemplated surrogacy, but has been too ill because she suffers from colitis. 'I feel I could have done it if the circumstances had been right,' she says. 'I honestly think I could have had a baby for someone else who couldn't have one. I can understand how deeply women who want children must feel because I feel so deeply the other way, that I don't want them.' It was Ilona's curiosity that led her to midwifery, and she estimates that she has attended over 300 births. 'Normally when you're nursing people are ill, but not when you're a midwife. I can enjoy that joyful feeling the mothers and fathers have at the end. I'm not frightened of giving birth,' says Ilona, 'having seen so many, I'd like to know the feeling of being pregnant, of having another life inside you. It must be interesting.' Although Ilona is confident that she and her husband don't want the responsibility of a child, there is a flicker of doubt. 'With surrogacy I always have in the back of my mind, would I be able to give it away? I feel as if I would, but you never know until you're in that situation.'

Although admitting that childbearing is a huge experience, the women perceived it as just one of many remarkable gifts that life has to offer. 'I believe there are many other experiences that can be equally or more significant, it depends on what sort of person you are and what you want out of life,' says Janet, 29. In the words of Coral: 'I just thought: that's another of the great feelings I'm never going to have in my life.' Although some women would like to have experienced childbirth, there was an overriding understanding that unlike a parachute jump or any other exhilarating life moment, this one delivered at least an 18-year commitment. They saw the responsibilities of motherhood as too high a price to pay, and in the words of Ruth, 'I've gained more by missing it than I've lost by not having it.'

Maternal instinct

But what about the maternal instinct? Isn't it only natural that women should want to have babies? This widespread view has to be tackled when discussing child-free women. Many of the interviewees have been accused of not fulfilling their 'natural' role, and some themselves questioned whether by not wanting children they were somehow 'unnatural'. The implication of such an idea is serious: that child-free women are going against the grain, that their denial will lead to unhappiness, lack of fulfilment and frustration. In other words, it is wrong for a woman to resist pregnancy, and in her best interest to have children.

Is biology our destiny? Many have thought so, stretching back in history to St Thomas Aquinas who wrote that animal judgement is not free but implanted by nature. We are, after all, part of the animal kingdom. Where animals are concerned there does seem to be a biological maternal instinct at work. Psychologist John Nicholson reports that virgin female rats show very little interest in other rats' pups, but they become much more maternal, building nests or retrieving pups when they wander off, when they are given a transfusion of blood taken from a rat which has recently given birth. 'This suggests that rats have a maternal instinct, and that it is under hormonal control,' writes Nicholson.[5]

Instinctive behaviour is seen as a driving force that comes from within, and psychologists have long argued about the existence of instinct as an aspect of human behaviour. Early theories attempted to identify a whole range of innate drives that can explain every aspect of human behaviour, whilst some modern psychologists have completely dismissed the notion of instinct as a meaningful concept, on the grounds that no part of human behaviour can ever be totally uninfluenced by learning and the environment. Two key figures emerged in the nature/nurture debate. In the 1920s William McDougall developed 'hormic psychology' which attempted to explain human behaviour as goal-seeking, and listed seventeen human instincts with an emotional core, including hunger, curiosity, sex, gregariousness, laughter, sleep and the maternal/paternal instinct. He believed that the emotional core of the latter was tender feeling. This psychological approach ranked humans along with animals, and was attacked by 'behaviourists', particularly John B. Watson, who stressed that it is learnt behaviour that propels us through life. The idea that the desire for maternity is biologically based is supported in part by research into genetic sex disorders. Children born with external female genitalia who are chromosomally and hormonally male may be raised as girls, and develop very traditional feminine identities, with the exception that they have little or no desire to have a child.[6]

Freudian psychoanalysts have taken a different approach, asserting that human behaviour grows out of the expression of a contrary set of instincts: the life instinct, which is basically a drive for sex; and the death instinct, which includes aggression. For Freud, however, 'anatomy is destiny' and shapes our psychological make-up. He believed that with the dawning awareness of sexual difference girls see their absence of a penis as lack. In

51

order to resolve their sense of missing something, they seek babies as a replacement. 'A woman's wish for a child is viewed not as a uniquely female drive, grounded in female biology, but as a displaced wish for the missing male penis,' explains psychologist Mardy Ireland.[7]

Jung differed from Freud's psychoanalytic theory when he asserted that the innate drive towards sex was more a general drive for life energy. Instead of seeing the maternal instinct as a drive towards procreation, Jung described it much more broadly as 'the mysterious root of all growth and change'.

In the 1950s leading psychologists dismissed the importance of instinct, arguing that no list of behaviour is totally free from the influence of learning: everything that we do is a product of both nature and nurture, and it is false and ultimately meaningless to try and make a sharp distinction between the two. But ideas of instinct became important once again in the work of psychologist Konrad Lorenz, who concluded in 1965 that humans have innate caring behaviour for their young, which is triggered by specific physical cues found in infants: the childlike large head, large eyes and rounded body.

Theories of biological determinism trap women, and the argument that women are free of the tyranny of genetics, and are governed instead by culturally determined behaviour, has been one of the great crusades of feminism during the past three decades. Philosopher Simone de Beauvoir first questioned the maternal instinct in 1949 when she described maternity as a woman's natural 'calling', but added that 'human society is never abandoned wholly to nature'.[8] Women have felt restricted by theories of biologically determined behaviour, and it has therefore been necessary for feminists to prove that we are governed instead by culturally determined behaviour. 'I don't believe that hormones are the most important thing. Feminism has taught me this, and it is so liberating,' says Marie, 44. 'A woman is so much more sophisticated than biology. The maternal instinct doesn't exist. It has been invented by men, I firmly believe that.'

One of the major arguments against the existence of maternal instinct is that if such an instinct exists it must be universal amongst all women, and impervious to the variability of cultures and history. If there is maternal instinct, why should a woman want to stop at 1.8 children, currently the national average in Britain? Should she not be driven by her biology to conceive again and again, taking her reproductive life to its absolute limit? Why have 3 million women chosen to have an abortion since the Abortion Act in 1967? Why, before the legalisation of abortion, did women threaten their own lives with tortuous backstreet abortions in an attempt to control their fertility?

Demographics has shown that there is a great variation in childbearing at times of social change. For example, in America during the Depression of the 1930s 20 per cent of married women had no children. By contrast in 1960 childlessness had dropped to 7 per cent.

French historian Elisabeth Badinter caused controversy when she published *The Myth of Motherhood* in 1980, an historical view of the maternal instinct.[9] Drawing on a plethora of literary and historic sources she argues that maternal love is not linked to nature because its manifestations throughout history are too varied to warrant the term 'instinct'. Badinter analyses motherhood in France during the eighteenth century, and discovers a very different attitude to the child-centred culture we have today. She argues that pre-1760 childhood was viewed negatively: an animal-like condition, easily corrupted by sinful influences. She quotes theologians and educators of the time: 'Childhood is the life of a beast'; 'Not only at the moment of our birth but even in our childhood we are like beasts without reason, language and judgment.' Badinter points to the absence of children in literature at that time, and also to the medical profession's lack of interest in children (specialisation in paediatrics only came about in 1872). She then goes on to examine the nature of the relationship between mother and child and uncovers a lack of interest which would have today's social workers frantically issuing care orders.

At the very beginning of its life, sometimes within the first few hours, most babies were taken away from their mothers and handed over to a wet nurse. Breast-feeding was thought to be physically bad for the mother, and consequently by the mid-eighteenth century city children nursed by their mothers were a rarity. Of 21,000 babies born in Paris in 1780 only 1,000 were nursed at home. The conditions in which wet nurses lived were often appalling, as they were usually poor, and society took so little interest in child welfare that there were no regulations to control their business. The infant mortality rate was staggering: a quarter of all babies died before their first birthday. The death of a child was apparently treated with some dispassion, and typically parents were absent from funerals of infants less than five years old. Perhaps lack of parental concern served merely as a form of self-protection? A mother might prevent herself from getting too attached to her baby for fear of likely bereavement. Badinter maintains that this view merely sustains our 'comfortable twentieth century views about motherhood', and claims that 'it was not so much because children died like flies that mother showed little interest in them, but rather because the mothers showed so little interest that the children died in such great numbers'. She quotes one wealthy woman as saying that nursing her child 'bores me, and I have better things to do'.

Taking this line of thought further: if maternal love is a universal given, why then did mothers in the eighteenth century treat their children with such inequality? There was usually a preference for the eldest son, which leads Badinter to ask: 'Doesn't this variability only affirm that love was above all a response to the possible social gain a child might represent?'

There is psychological research to back up Badinter's historical observations. Recent surveys have shown that only about half of all women feel an immediate sense of love for their babies. Four out of ten first-time mothers recall that their predominant emotion on holding their baby for the first time was indifference. A survey carried out in the Netherlands concludes that men and women can be just as happy without children as with them. Writes psychologist John Nicholson:

A large and representative sample of men and women between the ages of twenty-five and sixty-five answered questions about their satisfactions and fears, and their replies offered no support whatever for the view that having children is a recipe for happiness in either sex. Parents in the sample were no happier than non-parents – if anything, the reverse was true – and older people without children were found to be no more anxious about old age or death than those who had children, nor were they more doubtful about the purpose of life.[10]

Much as some would like to uphold theories against the maternal instinct, it does seem to be impossible to disprove or prove the case either way. We have a forceful and complex culture which at times can override our strongest instinctive behaviour. How otherwise would it be possible for prisoners to starve themselves to death in support of a political issue? Or a nun to forsake all sexual urges and join a religious community? The apparent lack of interest in motherhood in eighteenth-century France cannot rule out the maternal instinct completely. After all, the women were still having sex and having babies, which could be argued as the bottom line. Perhaps the most one can say is that if the maternal instinct does exist in humans it is fragile and easily overladen by cultural imperatives. 'The varied lives of women who aren't mothers support the idea that motherhood is more of a culturally embedded mandate than a biological or psychological mandate,' says Mardy Ireland. One must also ask how helpful it is to promote theories about human behaviour which are impossible to prove conclusively one way or another. Nature and nurture are ultimately inseparable, so the question about maternal instinct has to remain open. 'Since there is no convincing evidence that women are governed by instinct to have children, I think we should abandon the notion of maternal instinct, while acknowledging that the experience of being a mother is one which the great majority of women still prefer not to miss,' suggests Nicholson.

The interviewees had varying opinions about the existence of maternal instinct, and their views reflect the different positions taken by theorists. Some of the women

56

declared the maternal instinct a complete myth created by society to compel women to reproduce:

> It's probably conditioning from society. Also a great deal of women want to be needed, want something of their own, something that is dependent on them. It makes them feel wanted, loved and needed. Is this confused with a maternal instinct? (Jane, 29)

> I don't believe in the maternal instinct, it has been created by society. (Emily, 37)

> I think the maternal instinct is a complete con. All it means is that you sacrifice so much and end up with damn all at the end of it. You lose your career, years of pension, and these days there are so many divorces. He could go off and leave you, and then you've got nothing and these dependents hanging around your neck, and no one's going to help you. (Miriam, 33)

> I think it is something hyped by the media as if it is the ultimate and feminine thing for women to do. (June, 28)

Other women believe that we might be biologically driven towards procreation but that the force of this varies from woman to woman, and is influenced enormously by social conditions:

> Maybe it does exist, but it's certainly not universal: I certainly don't have it. (Charlotte, 34)

> I think maternal instinct exists. I've seen it amongst family and friends too often to doubt it. I've seen women who seem to merge almost completely with their babies, anticipating their every need, and knowing

57

WILL YOU BE MOTHER?

without being told what is the right thing to do. They devote their lives to their children, and find immense fulfilment in it. However, I don't think maternal instinct exists in every woman, or to the same degree in all those who do possess it. It's a character trait like any other, that some people have and some don't. Many people mistakenly assume that because some women do have it, then all women should have it, and should be castigated if they don't exhibit it. It's widely used as an excuse not to bother teaching women to care for their babies: if they're 'real' women they should know by instinct. It's also part of the reason why the child-free choice is rarely presented as a real option for women: all normal women are supposed to possess the maternal instinct and are made to feel inadequate if they do not. I don't see any need to deny the existence of maternal instinct as many feminists do, I just object to its portrayal as a universal trait. (Janet, 29)

There are certainly women, and I know a number of them, who have strong maternal feelings and just know they want children. Some have had babies on their own without marriage, because they want babies. I think it probably depends on the circumstances whether you want babies; on the relationship with the chap and how you see that. (Coral, 43)

You've either got it or you haven't! (Annabelle, 49)

I find small babies actually very ugly: they're all red and wrinkly and their eyes are half closed and they've got no hair. When they're older I think they're cute – like Muppet drawings, very sweet. I think that some women feel the maternal urge more strongly than others. Why are some people extrovert and some people introvert? Why anything? I'm sure it's partly conditioning, and my mother wasn't very maternal, although she seems to have developed now as a potential grandmother, which I think is hilarious, frankly. (Sue, 33)

I think an instinct exists to take care of small and vulnerable babies, but I wouldn't say there is anything instinctive and universal about the rest of the 'symptoms' of maternal instinct. (Jo, 39)

The baby button

Among some interviewees there was a perception that the 'maternal instinct' might suddenly develop and their conscious and considered decision not to have children would be overridden by an uncontrollable emotional desire to do so. It was imagined to be a force that could suddenly be turned on, as if at the press of a button, or the wave of a wand. 'It hasn't really happened yet. People always say it's going to happen soon, but I don't know when,' muses 26-year-old Elizabeth, who says she has never felt interested in motherhood. 'It hasn't happened yet. I can take babies or leave them.'

'I do worry that I might actually change my mind. You hear so much about the biological clock and how women suddenly want babies. Women who are mothers tell me that I don't know what it's like. I'm a bit suspicious about this, but I do worry that it might happen,' says Helen, 26. She thinks that her belief in a maternal instinct is partly informed by her mother, who was unable to have children and adopted Helen as a baby. 'I don't know the details about their infertility but it came across loud and clear to me that my mother was desperate to have children.' Helen, as a medical support worker on a gynaecology ward, has also come into contact with infertile women desperate to conceive. Likewise, Tunujah, 26, thinks, 'I don't feel a need to have a child at the moment, but I do get the feeling that one day I might start wanting them. Maybe when I get to a certain age. You do hear about women who are suddenly desperate to have children.' These women have decided against sterilisation as a contraceptive option because of a fear about the existence of a baby button.

This fear that a woman might suddenly be consumed with baby longings seems to fade with age. By the age of 40 most women felt that it was now extremely unlikely that they would find themselves chasing after prams. 'If it hasn't happened by now it's not going to,' states Liz, 40, who has now been sterilised and says she has never been interested in motherhood.

I thought there would be some magic thing that would happen to me,' says 40-year-old Phillippa, who has also now been sterilised. 'I've worked with so many girls and it's in them: "I'd love to have a baby." I never felt like that. I can't really explain why.'

The popular concept of the 'baby button' is one of the ways in which women are pressurised into having children: the 'well, I ought to have one, just in case I regret it later' philosophy. Psychiatrist Julian Hafner, writing in *The Times* in March 1993, describes it thus: 'The myth of a universal maternal instinct is unhelpful to women. It puts pressure on them to have children, and to then experience childbirth and child-raising as exclusively pleasant fulfilling events. The reality for most women is different.' The proof of the pudding is in the eating. If an innate breeding instinct means that true happiness for women can only lie in rocking a cradle, how can it be that so many mothers – up to a third, according to some estimates – suffer from depression? By contrast, resounding in my ears are the words of one child-free woman, Marie, a 44-year-old journalist who oozes *joie de vivre*: 'I'm so happy I haven't got children. I can't tell you how happy I am! My idea is that life is so rich, I have so many things to do, I can visit so many countries, learn so many languages, learn so many subjects: art, music, painting, read so many novels. There are so many wonderful human beings on earth, why would I want to dedicate myself to one single little one?'

3

THE MOTHER EXPERIENCE

THERE is an assumption that one does not need to learn how to be a mother, that the role is intrinsically rooted in woman's nature. Give her a baby and it will all somehow happen instinctively, magically. Mother love will know what to do.

John Watson, a founding father of behaviourist psychology, spent time observing young mothers with their babies, and concluded that nursing is the only activity that comes naturally. 'The mother is usually about as awkward as she can be. The instinctive factors are practically nil,' he writes. From the very first minutes of birth a woman is expected to bond with her child and love it immediately. Ideas about bonding have even extended to the womb, when the new legal category 'fetal abuse' was introduced in America: a husband prosecuted his wife for taking antibiotics while pregnant and thereby discolouring the child's teeth. Recent theories about pre-birth learning have encouraged mothers to communicate with an unborn child by talking to it, playing classical music and educational tapes. The mother/child relationship has been seen as crucial by psychologists, and failure of a mother to bond with a newborn child has been blamed for all types of delinquent behaviour. Psychoanalysis has greatly contributed to making the mother the centre of the family with the suggestion that an emotionally unhappy child is the son or daughter of a bad mother. There's scant mention of the father's role.

To be a bad mother has become the greatest of sins. Since the late eighteenth century and particularly during the Victorian era the good mother has been idealised. The modern view of motherhood developed as, in the words of psychiatrist Julian Hafner, writing in *The Times*:

> The Industrial Revolution and the associated warfare of the 18th and 19th centuries gained momentum. An endless supply of men and women was needed for factories and cannon fodder. Children became valuable commodities, and mothers became subject to propaganda urging them to take direct personal responsibility for their upbringing. Efforts by the state to increase the rate of population created incentives that enhanced the survival rate of infants and children. These incentives also included attempts to idealise motherhood, a process that was ultimately very successful.[1]

Elevated to an almost saintly role, the idealised mother is seen as self-denying, self-sacrificing and unconditionally loving. To question that she might be anything other than naturally loving sends shock waves deep into the collective psyche. The woman who does not love her child is hated and banished to the outskirts of society. 'Bitch!' screamed the tabloid headlines about Yasmin Gibson, a single mother, struggling actress and dancer, who left her 11-year-old daughter Gemma at home while she went on holiday to Spain. The case popularly became known as the 'Home Alone' story (after the successful box-office film of the same name) and made front-page news for several days in early 1993. There was little sympathy for this young woman who was herself the product of a dysfunctional family. The popular press was quick to capitalise on the emotional response aroused in readers about bad mothering. Tellingly, there was scant mention of Gemma's father, who had abandoned the family some time previously. Where were the headlines yelling 'Bastard'? It is bad mothering not bad fathering which arouses such hatred. But at a deeper level Yasmin Gibson arouses fear because she raises the question of whether our own mothers loved us. In the words of Elisabeth Badinter:

> In spite of our most open-minded intentions, the mother who does not love her child is still regarded as abnormal. We are prepared to explain away everything, to justify anything rather than to admit her within the range of normality. Deep down we are repulsed to think that mother love is not immune to all defects or variations of character . . . perhaps because we refuse to question what we prefer to believe is the absolute and unconditional love for us of our own mothers.[2]

Women have been striving to free themselves from the sole burden of childcare and trying to set it in a wider social context. Experts need to be criticised for neglecting to explore the importance of paternal bonding. 'Where is the phrase "paternal deprivation?" ' asks columnist Suzanne Moore in the woman's page of the *Guardian*.[3] A new generation of female psychologists has raised the issue of 'mother-blaming', explaining how, in clinical psychology, the mother is inevitably blamed for emotional problems in a child. She is branded as cold and rejecting, or over-protective. 'We need to ask ourselves why we automatically look to the mother. Why don't we assume that the father, alone or in addition to the mother, hasn't helped his child enough?' asks professor of applied psychology, Paula J. Caplan.[4]

Living up to the ideal

Against this background of the idealisation of motherhood and mother love, it is a brave admission for a child-free woman to state that she would not make what is generally thought of as a 'good mother', or for a mother to reveal that she has not matched up to the glorious ideal. Few women are prepared to admit that they regret having their children. No doubt these feelings are felt privately by some women, but they are rarely voiced, even in whispers. There has been a deafening silence about the reality of mothering, even amongst mothers, for fear of being branded as a bad mother, and thus a failure as a woman. Women cover up their feelings, to others and to themselves. 'For many women anything short of perfection begins to feel like failure and they become caught in a spiral of trying even harder to achieve the unachievable, and then becoming increasingly guilty with what they see as the worst failure of their lives,' says psychiatrist Jane Price.[5]

Research presented at the autumn meeting of the Royal College of Psychiatrists in 1986 demonstrated that up to

50 per cent of UK mothers with small children under the age of five have symptoms of intensive emotional distress on a regular or continual basis. Women are five times more likely to be diagnosed as mentally ill in the year after their first child's birth than at any other time in their lives. At least one in ten women suffers from post-natal depression, and more than half of those who are not treated are still depressed a year later. It is hard for women to articulate feelings which are in such stark contrast to the prevailing expectations of maternal bliss. They censor their negative feelings about mothering, and criticise themselves for having doubts and regrets. In our society mothering is supposed to be a happy event, and the arrival of children a cause for celebration. How is a mother supposed to equate this with a depression she feels about her new role? When compiling the book *Why Children?* in 1980,[6] editors Stephanie Dowrick and Sibyl Grundberg found women who were unhappy about being mothers, but none who were prepared to say so in print. Ten years on, there has been a spate of stories in women's magazines about the regrets that come with motherhood, a hopeful indication that women are gaining confidence in their self-worth outside of the attributed role of good mother. The past decade has seen the subject get a lot more airing, and a book has even been published on what is probably seen as the ultimate female transgression, abandoning a child, *Mummy Doesn't Live Here Anymore* by Helen Franks.[7]

Feminism has no doubt created a safe space in which discontents with mothering can be aired. In the first decades of the women's movement women fought for equality within the workplace, an ambition which seemed to exclude mothering. In January 1987 *Spare Rib* magazine reviewing attitudes to motherhood during the 1960s and 1970s, said:

> The issue became one of choosing, of what or who should be put first [job or home]. By deciding, as women, to put ourselves and our liberation first there was a feminist backlash against motherhood. The 'wife and mother' stereotype was forcefully rejected and child-bearing and rearing became 'unfashionable' in many feminist circles.

Childbearing had become a problem and an issue of debate for women: difficult feelings about maternity started to be explored honestly. Today, it has become possible for a major women's magazine to carry the following mother's testimony:

> It isn't that I don't love him [her baby] in my own way. I look at him when he's sleeping and objectively I can see how pretty and sweet he is. But I honestly don't experience the gut-wrenching sense of adoration that mothers are supposed to feel – and I can't cope with the idea of him dominating my life.[8]

Self-confessed 'bad' mothers

When asked whether they thought they had the skills, reserves and personal attributes to cope well with motherhood, many of the child-free women courageously admitted that they didn't. 'I am not patient, I am not tolerant, I am not practical, I don't think I have the energy, and I don't like doing things I'm not good at,' maintains Sally, 32. 'I am not sure I have enough love to give to another human being,' says Sandy, 35. 'I don't feel I'd be very good at giving children the time and enthusiasm that they need,' says Jo.

The women expressed myriad reservations, with their inability to cope with noise probably coming top of the list. 'I'd go mad with all that screaming and crying,' was a typical response. The prospect of small babies brought with it special alarm: 'I haven't a clue what to do with babies,' said one woman. Babies were seen as worrying agents of disruption – unpredictable and hugely resistant to routine, waking at unexpected hours, demanding food and clean nappies at inconvenient moments. 'Noise, mess, constant chaos – you name it,' says Janet. Many of the interviewees said that they didn't want the loss of control over their lives that babies and young children would inevitably bring, transforming the organised adult world into an enormous adventure playground. One woman, Marnie, had especially strong feelings about this which she attributed to the experience of having a schizophrenic older brother: 'All through my life I had to consider my brother and what I did. I remember silly little things like wanting to watch the television late and not being allowed to because then he would want to watch it, and then they wouldn't be able to get him up for work in the morning. Lots of things like that. I'm quite obsessive about having control over my life because I had so little when I was younger. I want to decide what I want to do. If you have a child you lose control.'

Some women believed that in reaction to chaos they might be over-zealous disciplinarians and make their children's lives a misery. 'I think I would be too strict,' says June, 28. 'I would be hard on the kids, as I like things done my way when I want them done,' says Georgina, 32. At its most extreme, two women expressed concern that they might abuse a child if their nerves became overwrought. No one knows how many children are cruelly beaten and abused, as for the most part it happens behind closed doors. The Department of Health suggests that in 1990 28,200 children were in need of protection. Babies under one are four times as likely as any other age group to be murdered.

For the past eighteen years the National Society for the Prevention of Cruelty to Children has been studying the stress factors which lead to abuse, and has discovered a complex web of interrelated causes which, says Christopher Brown, director of the NSPCC, 'relate to the needs and behaviour of the child, the characteristics of the parent, and environmental factors such as housing, unemployment and debt'.[9] According to an NSPCC report of 1988–90, parents of registered children were much less likely to be in paid employment than parents nationally, with over half the families in receipt of income support. Debt was also found to be a major factor, along with poor, cramped housing. The report gives a detailed sociological profile, but for psychological profiles one has to look elsewhere.

Estela Welldon, a psychiatrist and psychotherapist, has written about women who mistreat their children. She believes they often see children as an extension of themselves, and that injury to the child is a form of self-punishment by proxy. The idealisation of the role of motherhood prevents this problem being recognised. How could a woman possibly want to harm her children? Isn't such action directly in conflict with her inborn nature? Says Welldon:

Mothers are expected by society to behave as if they had been provided with magic wands which not only free them from previous conflicts, but also equip them to deal with the new emergencies of motherhood with skill, precision and dexterity. Why is it so difficult for us to see that, for some women, motherhood intensifies their previous problem to the point where they are unable to cope anymore?[10]

There is a growing awareness that 'settling down' into a family is not necessarily a cure-all for life's problems, but can in fact intensify difficulties. In the words of French psychoanalyst Jacques Lacan: 'The nuclear family is a hotbed for the production of neuroses.'[11] The demand for counselling and family therapy has increased as awareness of psychological problems has risen, spawning books like the bestseller *Families and How to Survive Them*, written by John Cleese and his psychiatrist Robin Skynner. Skynner says of parents who batter their children:

> [They] tend to be extremely needy. I have found that they generally have had harsh childhoods themselves and they have a great need for their children to love them. They have low self-esteem so that if the child starts crying for hours, they feel an acute sense of failure and can suddenly flip and fling the child against the wall.[12]

As a child, Miriam, now 33, believed that she was unwanted and resented by her parents: she was frequently beaten and neglected. 'Once they had me they discovered they'd made a horrible mistake,' she explains. Her parents had been married for nineteen years and had chosen not to have children. Miriam believes that they were 'bribed' to start a family by her mother's older brother and father-figure. It became obvious that his own children weren't going to have children, and desperate to become a grandparent, he decided he'd like to be a 'grand-uncle' instead. 'He put the screws on my mum and dad by taking them on a massive pub crawl. He was very intelligent and had made a lot of money on the stock market in America. He offered them money, got them blind drunk and they agreed. It was a mistake. I disrupted things for them and was just a nuisance. My mum was a party animal and couldn't go out and party like she used to. They didn't have any money any more and could only go on self-catering holidays. They said they didn't row until I came along. Apparently I was always crying and they used to shove me down the end of the garden in the pram so they couldn't hear me. They disliked having me around so much there was absolutely no possibility that another child would be welcomed at all. The idea was unthinkable, it was so obviously a total mistake.' Miriam remembers being left to her own devices for most of her childhood. 'I started going on long walks and cycle rides, anything to get away.' She says she was beaten because her parents thought her clumsy – 'My mum used to beat the living daylights out of me' – and it was only when she was seven that the problem was diagnosed as short-sightedness.

Miriam married at 19, and although she didn't expect to have children, the possibility wasn't completely ruled out until she had a serious road accident later that same year and suffered a long period of depression, during which she was aggressive and violent towards her husband. 'I took to throwing things at him and attacking him,' she remembers. 'It brought it home to me that I was aggressive and would probably be a bad parent. I've hit pets and things like that. One time the cat kept waking me and waking me, and I couldn't sleep. I caught the cat, grabbed it by the throat and dunked it in the washing-up bowl. I came to the conclusion it wouldn't be unlike me to beat a kid the same way as I was beaten when I was a child. I'm worried I'd beat a child into a pulp; when my temper goes I absolutely blow. I'm not good parenting material.'

Julia, 32, similarly felt that her temper was too volatile for parenthood: 'Given enough provocation I would make the headlines for child abuse or possibly manslaughter. I'm not a violent person under normal circumstances, but I have no difficulty in imagining myself being driven over the edge by screaming, whining children.'

Miriam and Julia confessed to a potentially extreme adverse reaction to parenthood, but they shouldn't be singled out as wholly deviant: numerous other interviewees, although not anticipating that they would harm children, expressed fears about how overwrought they might be made by childcare. Considering that parenting is so taxing, this is hardly surprising. The situation also seems to be getting worse: in an NSPCC poll, 85 per cent of parents reported being under more stress now than five years ago, and 55 per cent admitted to 'over-reacting' to their children's behaviour.[13]

Society does not readily accept responsibility for children, and instead encourages parents, usually the mother, to do all the hard work. It spells out in a romanticised way what it thinks 'good mothering' should be, yet provides little practical support. In fact, society can be downright hostile to women with children. The built environment is notoriously child-unfriendly as any woman who has tried to get on and off a crowded bus with a baby-buggy will testify. Working women are constantly asking for improved state childcare, requests which have so far fallen on deaf ears. Mothers receive no payment for their toil, and worst still the job of mothering is dismissed as boring and unskilled. 'What is missing in the understanding of mothering is the extent to which it is a painful relationship and an exhausting, often thankless, occupation . . . . Of the many women I see in counselling, I am struck by the normality of the psyches and the ridiculous nature of the demands placed upon them,' writes Jane Price, NHS consultant and co-editor of *Motherhood: A Feminist Perspective*.[14]

We all need time alone for good mental health, something which mothers rarely have because of the 24-hour demands children make. Some interviewees felt that they would regret this loss of personal space. Marnie again: 'I don't like the idea of waking up the next morning after giving birth and having this other human life that's so dependent on you, that has to be with you the whole time. I don't think I want to be with somebody the whole time. I like space and enjoy time on my own; a couple of nights a week at least.' Janet, 29, agrees: 'For me the most difficult thing about being a parent would be the sense of suffocation I would experience at being irrevocably tied to a helpless and totally dependent being. I've heard mothers say that this has inspired a tremendous sense of awe and increased self-worth in them, but for me it would be like being in prison. A child is endlessly needy and demanding, and whether it is physically present or not, emotionally the mother must be on call 24 hours a day. I would feel totally consumed by a child's needs, unable to function as an individual. I'm a private person, and with a small child there is little privacy. I enjoy my solitude; the constant physical presence of a dependent child would have me screaming in no time.'

Support from partners

Many women commented on the sheer hard work that comes with being a mother, and worried about coping. 'I didn't think I'd be able to . . . . I've always had difficulty coping with life; getting the necessary things done. It's bad enough if it's only oneself, only one's own things that get neglected, but if you've got young children wanting to be fed, washed, it would get into a real mess,' says Lucy, 69.

Studies have suggested that mothers with young children suffer higher levels of exhaustion than any other group, especially working women. The interviewees recognised that because of the failure to achieve all of the demands of feminism, we live in a difficult trans-formational period: although we have claimed our right to equality in the workplace, equality in the home is lagging far behind. Men have been slow to assume joint responsibility for domestic tasks and childcare, and as a consequence women who are in their twenties, thirties and forties are perplexingly divided: one foot is in the expanding world of paid employment, and the other foot is still rooted in the domestic world their mothers inhabited. The tension is apparent in the spread of terminology like 'supermum', 'burn-out' and 'having it all'. When the 1987 British Social Attitudes Survey asked couples to say which partner was mainly responsible for general domestic duties, 82 per cent said the woman and only 12 per cent said that the chores were shared equally. Men were more likely to claim an equal division than women. In 88 per cent of homes where the man worked full-time and the woman part-time, it was still the woman who did most of the housework and, appallingly, the same was also true of 72 per cent of families where both partners worked full-time. 'Bridging the divide between men and women to create a truly equitable public and private world is likely to take a very long time,' warns Kathleen Kiernan, research director of the Family Policy Studies Centre.

Some women were unwilling to become the victims of this inequality. 'My older brother tried to get me into the kitchen to stand next to my mother and learn to cook, but I really resisted. I don't want to be the little homemaker whilst daddy goes to work. I'm only interested in men who would share the domestic life, and there aren't many men of my age like that in the Asian community,' says Tanujah. Says Ruth, 56: 'If I'd been a man I wouldn't have minded having children, but being a woman I'd resent having all the responsibility.'

Over-anxious

Some women worried that they would make anxious mothers who were over-protective of their children. They anticipated that they might smother a child with their concern, something which psychiatrists report to be as potentially damaging as lack of parental care. 'I'm sure I'd be too anxious for their welfare and have difficulty in letting them go their own way,' says Julia, 32. 'I wouldn't be relaxed enough to cope.' Annabelle, 49, agrees: 'I'd worry or panic about everything.' Phillippa, 40, watched how her sister dealt with motherhood and recognised behaviour that she saw as potentially within herself:

75

'I don't think I'd be able to cope, letting a young child of mine go out in this world. I'd have to go everywhere with them. My little sister went through the same – she couldn't let her little boy go to school and he didn't even have to cross the road. She went and talked to her doctor about it in the end, and had to force herself to let him go. Even then she used to watch him out of the window. I would be a hundred times worse than that.'

It may be sad that these women's decisions not to have children are based so much on negative factors: they have assessed the attributes needed for parenthood and found themselves lacking. It's difficult to quantify how much of a deciding factor 'I'm bad mother material' is when choosing to remain child-free. Perhaps if a woman really wants a child she will have one, no matter how many doubts she has about her abilities to cope? There is probably a lot of truth in 34-year-old Patricia's statement: 'Would I make a good mother? No, because I don't wish to be one.' We need to honour the process these women have gone through, their self-examination and honest appraisal of character, and refrain from criticism. After all, everyone can't be good at everything. Their self-criticism indicates the high esteem in which they hold the job of mothering, and how valuable and deserving they believe children to be. 'I think so much of children and what a precious thing it is you're doing when you bring a life into the world,' says Karen, 36. 'What a responsibility – to nurture this life so it will emerge into a balanced human being. It's an enormous responsibility that I don't feel equal to. I don't see myself in that role and am fearful that I can't do that job well enough. I feel that people go into parenthood without any thought at all.'

If parenthood were seen more as an option in life, rather than an inescapable event, perhaps more women would feel able to question their suitability for mother-hood. The British Organisation of Non-Parents (BON) produces a leaflet entitled *Am I Parent Material?*, listing thirty-two questions under the headings: 'What sort of parent would I be?', 'Would a child fit into my way of life?', 'What do I expect to gain from the experience of being a parent?' and 'Have I fully discussed becoming a parent with my partner?' These are searching questions indeed, and need to be asked by more people before they embark on parenthood. Perhaps if we first honestly assessed our ability to raise children there would be happier, healthier families? It's a possibility.

Good enough mothers

A minority of women felt that they did have the qualities needed to make good mother material. Quite what a 'good mother' is has to be open to debate, considering the stresses and difficulties that come with the role. Psychiatrist Jane Price suggests that women should instead be thinking of themselves as 'good enough' mothers. 'For many women anything short of perfection begins to feel like failure,' she says. To chase the idea of being nothing but a good mother is 'trying to achieve the unachievable'.[15]

'I think I would be caring and nurturing and all of those things women are meant to be. But I'd be aware that I was giving the children time and energy that I would want to have for myself. I don't think I'd be a bad mother, but I wouldn't be very tolerant,' considers 29-year-old Maria. 'I would be loving and very aware and sensitive,' says

Vicky, 37. Many of these women had been told by others that they had good mothering qualities. 'People used to say to me, "I can't understand why you don't have children because you like children so much",' says Ilona, 43, who spends a lot of time with her eleven godchildren. 'They say to me I have a lot of patience, but it's easy to be patient when you know you've only got the child to look after for so long. You can spoil them and spend time playing with them knowing you haven't got the rest of the day to cope with them.'

Attitudes towards children

It would be a mistake to think that women who don't want to become mothers necessarily dislike children. The broad question 'Do you like children?' is a dubious one: no one can adore children's behaviour at all times. Like adults, they can be loving, charming, entertaining, creative, as well as attention-seeking, selfish, demanding and cruel. 'It just depends on the child,' says Marnie, a teacher who works with special needs children. Karen, a musician, points out that if she finds the parents agreeable, she'll usually like their children too. 'Completely unruly, I think it's called "free-expression" children drive me daft, but then I'm inevitably not on the same wavelength as the parents either.'

Nevertheless, children have unique qualities, and their absence is increasingly being felt by some parts of adult society. 'Rediscover the child in you' has now become a familiar theme in personal growth therapies, which encourage adults to recover spontaneous creativity, free expression of emotion and a sense of wonder at the world. People often say that being with children brings out the child in them, makes them feel whole and mentally healthy. The popularity of workshops where adults rediscover their child-self could be a reaction to the fact that with the breakdown of the extended family and a declining birth rate, some adults have no contact at all with children.

Many of the interviewees said that their lives benefited from the presence of children and that they actively seek their company. Child-free women often make devoted aunts and godmothers, the role enabling them to enjoy a child's company without the responsibilities that jeopardise their adult lifestyle. Karen and her husband spend a lot of time with their godchildren. 'It's just something I feel like doing. No duty, no pressure. It's fun to be with them and have a rough and tumble, but I've never thought wouldn't it be lovely to do it with a child of my own.' Philippa and her husband have seventeen nieces and nephews whom they see regularly, and in their work as coach drivers they like children as passengers. 'There are a lot of coach drivers who won't take children,' explains Phillippa. 'One, because they don't give tips; two is that they're messy and noisy. We're the only couple in this company who will take the children, because we love them. They're so easily pleased and the money isn't that important to us.'

A couple of women have much younger siblings and half-siblings whose company they enjoy, like Siobhan, 30, who has a six-year-old half-brother. 'I do respond to children. I find myself talking to children on the street,' she says. 'I like the fact it's easy to share a laugh and a joke. They'll say things that are really off the wall. I love the way they look at the world. I can see the enjoyment but don't want the responsibility of bringing up my own.'

Some women work with children, mostly as teachers and nurses. Jo, 39, is an advisory teacher for young deaf children: 'I am easy and comfortable with them, and have had enough experience with them to make them feel at ease. I like their cuteness and innocence.' By teaching, she can enjoy their company, without 'the burden of a lifelong responsibility. Also I have free time and enough money to do the things I enjoy.' Louise, 34, the deputy head of a school for children with learning difficulties, says that she derives 'great pleasure from the children's achievements without having the 24-hour-a-day, seven-day-a-week commitment.'

By contrast, quite a few women said they dislike children. Some actively avoid contact with them. 'There are no children at all in my life, I'm so glad to say,' said one. 'I like nothing about children. They are noisy and demanding,' says another. Linda, 34, recently married, is visited by her husband's 10-year-old son one weekend a month. She finds 'tolerating children a real effort', and when asked, could think of nothing she likes about them. Sally, 32, agrees: 'They can be cruel to each other, jealous, greedy, selfish, loud. They usually ignore their parents and can be horrible towards pets.'

Which comes first: not getting on well with children, or disliking children? It's probably a chicken and egg scenario, but certainly the two go hand in hand. The women who felt they don't like children were also likely to say that they find it hard to relate to them. While describing why she finds children unpleasant, Debbie, 34, also slips in that they *embarrass* her, presumably because of some awkwardness she feels in their presence: 'I dislike their noise mostly. Their stupid computer games, jammy fingers and snotty noses. The way they want me to join in their games and then try to embarrass me. I really can't stand kids that grizzle and whine, and keep pestering their parents for sweets or whatever.' Janet, 29, says that she finds children and the games they want to play boring: 'I dislike their helplessness, their utter dependence on someone else for their existence. I find this suffocating, it doesn't inspire protective urges in me. I hate the noise and mess they generate, and the complete lack of peace and privacy that comes with having them around. I dislike the self-centredness of children, especially young ones, their idea that the world revolves around them, and everyone else exists to do their bidding. They want constant attention, but the things they want to do are incredibly dull. The company of children bores me silly after a very short time.'

These women value adult conversation and feel they can relate better with older children where there is an intellectual dynamic to the communication. 'I prefer the company of older children. Young children are totally inarticulate, they're a bundle of needs and wishes. They're untrained and uneducated,' says Marie, 44. Amelia, 22, agrees: 'I like children who are intelligent enough to enjoy being spoken to in an adult way.'

Attitudes to babies ranged from repulsion and horror, to indifference and adoration. 'When I was ten I had a fantasy when I walked home from school and saw these babies left outside the supermarket. I thought I'd snatch one, not to keep it, but to kill it,' admits Katrin, 27. Sue, 33, says she thinks small babies are physically unattractive, and jokingly refers to them as 'carpet monkeys'. Jane, 29, has eight nieces and nephews who range in age from 2 to 13, and says her interest in them grows as they grow, but she was aloof from them at the

81

baby stage. 'It's the older children whom I get along best with. I've never wanted anything to do with any of them as infants, and it has been rather painfully obvious at times that I'm the only one not crowing around the babies, begging to nurse them.' Conversely Maria, 29, feels quite passionate about newborns: 'I've held my sister's baby. I think babies are quite sweet. I find them amazing and intriguing. I remember seeing her, this little being in an incubator, and just fell in love.'

Little parents

Many Western young woman have little real idea about the practical responsibilities of mothering. With the breakdown of the nuclear family and the move towards families with smaller numbers of children, it's not uncommon for a woman never to have held a baby. 'The shock of motherhood seems to be a peculiarly Western phenomenon,' says journalist and mother Brigid McConville:

> Just as we have lost contact with the realities of death in our society, so we have removed birth from the family home and neighbourhood midwife and made it into a hospital affair to be dealt with by distant professionals. By contrast, many children of the developing world learn what it's all about as they mother their own baby brothers, sisters and cousins. Today's women are perhaps as sheltered from the facts of motherhood as our grandmothers were from the 'facts of life'.[16]

Yet the mystique of happy families continues and for those who've had no experience of small children, it is easy to take on the dream. A few of the interviewees, however, have had first-hand experience of caring for young children, because of younger siblings or stepbrothers/sisters. The role of being a 'little parent' was cited as one of the deciding factors in the choice to remain child-free. For these women the mystique of happy parenting has been blown apart.

Angie, 27, a black woman who works as a West End spotlight operator, comes from a home where her mother separated from her father when she was three. She was brought up in Birmingham by her maternal grandmother until the age of seven, while her mother went to London to train as a secretary and save for a flat. When Angie was 19 her mother remarried and had another daughter. Soon after Rachael's birth, Angie's new stepfather left the family, and her mother once again had to cope alone with a small child. Angie feels that her mother's life has been a struggle, and remains one. 'All those sleepless nights my mother had,' remembers Angie sadly. 'I'd try and relieve her when I could and go down at three in the morning for my sister. But I could always cut off, it wasn't my duty. I had that choice, to offer to help or stay in bed. It's probably affected me. Rachael could have been my child agewise. I had people mistake Rachael for my own child, and was quick to correct them. I didn't want people to think I'd got trapped by a teenage pregnancy like so many of the other girls at my school.'

Katrin, 27, who was born in East Germany, also found herself taking on responsibility for childcare because of her father's absence. Her parents divorced when she was 10, and she and her two younger sisters were raised by their mother. 'That's probably the main reason why I don't want children,' says Katrin, 'because I had to take care of my sisters when I was very young. After my parents' divorce my mother had to go to work all day, so I had to look after my sisters. I had all these house duties: cleaning, shopping, washing, cooking. I had a long way to walk to school: it would take about three-quarters of an hour. School finished at one o'clock, but younger children could stay until four o'clock. Because I had to walk my sisters home along a busy road I had to stay there until four o'clock. I hated it. I wasn't supposed to be there with all these small children.'

In large families, older siblings can also find themselves taking responsibility for younger ones. Trudy, 31, comes from a family of seven, with a gap of fourteen years between herself and her youngest sibling. 'I used to help feed them and dress them. When I was 11 or 12 I used to take them off mum's hands for the day and take them to the zoo or forest. Sometimes I think, well, I looked after them, and don't mind cuddling my nephews and nieces, but that's as far as it goes. I don't like babies and nappies.'

Katy, 23, is also much older than her younger brother. 'My mum and dad were planning on me and my older brother leaving home, and then Lee came along unexpectedly. I was 15 when he was born. I think initially they were shocked: my mum was using the coil. When the doctor told her she just sat there shaking, saying, "What am I going to do?" They were worried about how they would afford it as my dad's job wasn't that secure at the time. I would look after Lee for whole days during my school holidays when my mum was at work. They demand constant attention and it's a terrible drain on your energy.' She was often mistaken for his mother. 'I remember once I went for a job in a motorbike shop, and had my little brother in a pushchair. This guy was saying, "I think you should consider your responsibilities", and

I thought, what's he on about? Then it twigged: he thought Lee was my son. I said, "It's my brother", and eventually he gave me the job.'

Although she found this amusing, the role of surrogate mother changed her vision of life. 'I used to imagine living on a bus and having eight children. It was such an idyllic thing, having all these well behaved children around me. My brother made me realise all the responsibility involved. You've got to be prepared to give an awful lot, and they become the main part of your life. I started to think that maybe I didn't want that for myself.' Katy now works as an administrator for a nuclear power plant, and is an active member of the Baptist Church. Her husband recently had a vasectomy.

Stepmother

With one in three marriages ending in divorce and high remarriage rates it is not unusual for people to find themselves becoming stepparents. In 1988 only 63 per cent of marriages were between couples who had never married previously. 'Hybrid' families bring their own special problems, and many of the interviewees expressed reservations about committing themselves to a man who has children from a previous relationship. The women said they would miss their child-free lifestyle if the child was to live with them. 'If I'd wanted children in my life I would have had my own. Why should I take on someone else's?' sums up their attitude.

While it is extremely rare for a husband to retain custody of a child after divorce – 98 per cent of children live with their natural mothers – access frequently involves men in weekend parenting. Helen, 26, has a husband with a six-year-old daughter from a previous relationship. The little girl lives with her mother but 'I have nightmares about her turning up at the doorstep,' says Helen. The few women who were prepared to take on their partner's children were conscious that the role was fraught with difficulties. One consideration is that in custody battles stepmothers have few legal rights, which makes it hard for a woman to love and accept a child who might later be taken away from her. Trudy, a 31-year-old catering manager from the West Country, became a stepmother when she married in her early twenties. Her husband's son and daughter were 11 and 5 respectively. 'Their mother didn't want them because she had moved abroad and wanted to get on with her life,' explains Trudy, who says she loves children but has never felt driven to have one of her own. 'I wanted to be a good stepmother to them, somebody they could come home to and share their problems with. I loved them and treated them as if they were my own. Initially we used to get on really well and did things together as a family, then their mother came heavily back on the scene wanting access to the children. I never held back from letting them go to her, but when they came back they wouldn't speak to me.' Things got worse: 'My stepdaughter started to play off one against the other and my stepson got into trouble with the police for causing damage at his school.' Trudy, like her husband, had a career in the Air Force at the time which she decided to give up so that she could devote more time to the children. 'I thought I'd come out and be a better mother to the children while they're still growing up.'

Six years into her marriage, Trudy and her husband divorced. 'He started going away a lot and at the back of my mind I think he went off with somebody else.' Trudy is still pained by the divorce proceedings: 'I was made to sound like an evil stepmother. I was supposed to be really wicked and never let the children laugh in front of the television, always chose where we went on holiday, didn't let their friends come around the house. None of it was true.' She now has no legal right to see the children. 'The children went with him, and it was such a wrench because I thought I'd done my best for them. Now I don't have contact with them at all.'

The experience of still-birth

One woman's experience of maternity led to an extraordinary change of heart. Phillippa, a 40-year-old coach driver from Scotland, married her husband Ivan when she was 22, and although children weren't much discussed, there was an assumption that they would eventually start a family 'but I wasn't obsessed with it like some women are today,' says Phillippa. The couple didn't seriously start thinking about children until Phillippa was 25. 'I heard that somebody went in to have a baby and at 25 they were classed as an old mother. I thought if we do want them we'd better start thinking about it.' Despite her anxiety about time running out, Phillippa waited another three years before she and her husband started trying for a baby. 'We planned it so much that ten minutes after making love I just knew I'd conceived. I can't explain how. I felt OK being pregnant. I was quite pleased when the doctor told me the test was positive. My husband went out and bought me presents and all sorts of things. It was definitely wanted at the time.'

Six and a half months into the pregnancy Phillippa started to feel anxious that something had gone wrong. 'I knew it had died but nobody would listen to me. Even the doctors were saying don't worry, all mothers worry. It was my midwife who got concerned and got me to go for a scan when I was eight months. The doctor told me there and then that the baby was dead. I felt sick at first, although I had known. It was knowing that somebody is going to die but when it does happen you're still a little bit shocked. Although I had this feeling that something was wrong I kept hoping that everybody else was right and were going to prove me wrong.'

Phillippa went through the ordeal of an induced labour which lasted 26 hours and three shifts of nurses. 'It was terrible. What was really hurtful about it was the fact that I had to go through it all and nothing at the end of it. It was a breech birth, a little girl.'

Although distraught, Phillippa also felt peculiarly relieved. 'It was a weight off my shoulders,' she says. 'I wish I could have had somebody to talk to who had been through it. I didn't know how I should be feeling. I thought, why aren't I feeling suicidal? I was feeling OK. It was worse for my husband than me. He was terrible, really distraught. My midwife had to leave the room because he was on his hands and knees in grief.'

After the stillbirth, Phillippa postponed trying to conceive for four years. Each time she went to have a coil fitted her doctor would gently suggest that she might feel ready to try for another baby. 'Then one Sunday it was cold and my husband and I had a big dinner and were slouching about. I said, "Oh I could just do with 40 winks" and he said, "So could I." Then I thought, God, if I had a family I wouldn't be able to do this. I turned to my husband and said, "Do you really want a family?" I said, "I need you to answer this honestly." When he said he would be happy with or without, that's when I made my decision. It was the first time in my life I realised I had a choice. It would be up to me. It was the biggest and best decision I've ever made. I decided that I wouldn't have any, and it was like a ton of bricks that had come off my shoulders.'

Phillippa finds it hard to explain what had changed since the time she had conceived. 'I kept thinking that suddenly I would want to have a baby, like some magic thing happening to me. But I never felt like that. I'm just so pleased we haven't got any children for a mixture of reasons. I think the length of time we'd been together was important. A lot of people would call it selfish, but I call it set in our ways; that contributed to the fact.' Phillippa's anxiety about being over-protective also contributed to her decision. Four years after making this decision, Phillippa had problems with the coil and was sterilised, an option she hadn't realised was available to her. 'It was the answer to my prayers. Why didn't someone offer this to me before? I felt wonderful afterwards. A pregnancy won't stop me doing anything I want to.' Cynics might suggest that Phillippa did want another baby, but feared a further bereavement. She says not, and the acid test is her own satisfaction: 'We are so happy, that's how I know it was the right decision.'

Child substitutes

Some of the women said they had found other outlets for what they identify as 'motherly feelings'. 'My clients are my babies. Actors are very demanding and need a lot of attention,' says Elizabeth, theatrical agent. 'They need their egos massaging, they need pampering and telling that they're wonderful. A lot of them are quite insecure and when they don't get jobs it's a big knock to their confidence.'

For the past three years Marion, 41, has been living with her boyfriend Greg, nineteen years her junior. 'Interestingly enough I have a maternal urge. I act like Greg's mother,' she says. 'I listen to how mums talk to their sons and that's exactly the way I talk to Greg. Around the time of my late thirties I started to find myself really attracted to young men. Maybe I've sublimated my maternal urge, and it has now manifested itself in a desire for a younger man. As I was getting older my boyfriends were getting younger. I just baby Greg, always fussing, "Put your coat on" or "Have you got this or that?". It's a role I've slipped into: I don't like it at all. I think it's silly. He's a grown adult and goes out to work.'

It's probably true that unmarried women without children have a lot more time and energy to devote to others, and are valued for their availability, although this might also be taken for granted in some circumstances. Dianne, 28, a charity worker, says that she often gives friends emotional support when they go through a personal crisis. 'Sometimes I feel like I mother my friends or that I'm an agony aunt to them,' she says good-humouredly.

There is a popular stereotype that women without children are inordinately fond of pets and that their animals serve as 'child substitutes', but pets are also kept and adored by people with children. One infertile woman I met, who desperately wants children, showed me her two well-kept cats, saying that she spoils them terribly and treats them like children. However pets featured strongly in only a small number of interviews, a trend seemingly backed by American sociologist Jean Veevers who, in 1980 interviewed 156 couples who are child-free by choice. 'Only a small minority openly admitted that their pets were child surrogates,' says Veevers. In fact she discovered that child-free couples often disliked pet ownership and any experience of it reinforced their decision not to have a family. 'For most childless couples for whom animals were a factor in their decision making, the acquisition of a pet on a trial basis [had] the result that they were even less inclined towards the parenthood role.'[17] All the women who said they lavished affection on companion pets also made it clear that they didn't overly humanise their animals. 'I think some women have more maternal instinct than others. I don't deny I have some, but mine is, I admit, directed towards animals, more particularly my dog. But my dog is not my "baby": she is a dog,' states Julia.

Phillippa and her husband have a 20-year-old cat. Phillippa says she adores the animal and refuses to put it in a cattery because of its age. She's conscious that people might think of her cat as a child substitute, but maintains that this isn't the case, even though she describes the cat as being 'one of the family.' 'I've got a friend who can't have kids and I've watched the way she talks to her two cats. Although I love my cat I honestly would not talk to her like that. I've told my husband I'm never going to have another cat, it's too much of a worry.'

Julia said she feels more affinity with animals than children: 'I don't believe the maternal instinct exists in humans. Surely it's possible to be born without an "instinct" as I have been? I don't go around gazing fondly into prams or patting toddlers on the head, but I can't

91

resist stroking cats and dogs. Child-free people who keep pets are often accused of having sublimated desire to have kids; the patter of tiny paws being a substitute for the patter of tiny feet. I simply prefer cats to children.' Tanujah feels similarly, and jokes, 'I wish I could have kittens rather than babies; I'd much rather give birth to kittens.'

Adoption

Many women casually mentioned the option of adoption should they ever change their mind about not having children but find it too late for pregnancy. None of them had seriously investigated the possibility, and adoption probably has only a symbolic value for them, as an emotional safety net: 'If I do suddenly find myself craving babies this could be a possibility.' In reality, this option is highly unlikely due to the age limit for adoptive parents and the acute shortage of infants in Britain. For every ten couples who wish to adopt there is only one available baby. Parents have to go through a strict selection procedure and if they are successful it is not unusual to then have to wait up to three years. The waiting lists for some adoption agencies have closed. Many of the people who expressed an interest in adoption assumed they could easily get a child from another country. However, 'You need time, determination and money, about £5–15,000 to adopt from abroad,' said Susan Rice, chairperson of ISSUE, the self-help group for the infertile. 'There's no agency in this country to deal with inter-country adoptions, so you have to find your own way and be really determined to get through all the procedures and obstacles.'

It is slightly easier to adopt older children but, in the words of Rice, 'It's more difficult in that you're taking on a child with a difficult background. There's a lot of history there you'd have to deal with. Like infertility: everyone assumes they can have a child and get a shock when they find out they can't. The same with adoption: everyone assumes they can adopt and it's a shock when they find out they can't.'

Daily we see television pictures of children living in poverty and war-torn countries. Some of the women had a global sense of responsibility and felt that remaining child-free was selfish when there were so many children in need of loving homes. 'I wouldn't mind adopting a child. I have a very selfish independent life. When I read the tragic condition of children in ex-Yugoslavia, I think, why don't I take a child?' says Marie, a 44-year-old journalist, with a very comfortable, elegant home in west London. 'I have "adopted" a little girl in Colombia through a charitable group: I send her £20 a month. She's about eight, sends me cards, is very bright and doing well at school. I speak Spanish and plan to go to Colombia to see her and try to convince her to go to university. I will pay for her. At the moment she wants to be a nurse: why doesn't she become a doctor?' 'There are enough kids out there who don't have the natural love of their parents,' says Tanujah. 'I would rather foster or adopt than bring one of my own into the world.'

Helen, 26, was adopted as a baby and says that she feels 'in debt' to provide an unwanted child with the type of happy home she was fortunate enough to be brought up in. 'The world is so overpopulated, and it would be wrong to bring a child into the world,' she says. It is often assumed that parents do not love adopted children as much as their natural offspring. Helen has no doubt that she would fully love an adopted child: 'It seriously pisses me off to hear people say, "She's only an adopted child." I know how much I love my mum and dad and especially my dad. I couldn't imagine loving a natural parent any more than that. If I adopted a child I would love it like my own, I'm sure of it.'

Life eternal?

Children remind us of our passage from birth to death, and can trigger spiritual questions about life's meaning. Emily, 22, a Catholic who occasionally attends church, says, 'They look so perfect in my arms my eyes start watering. I get overcome with emotion. I like imagining how amazingly they grow into a huge human being. Isn't it miraculous?' I remember a sermon in which a priest spoke of a man who had a dramatic religious conversion after witnessing the birth of his child. Such emotional moments often lead to contemplation of life's deeper meanings. For many people children symbolise hope and affirm the continuation of the species. They make the thought of death less difficult to bear. We live in a culture that has sadly lost the art of commemorating death. Death is hidden, nailed down quickly in coffins lest we catch sight of the body. Funerals have become unceremonious affairs that are raced through in half-hour slots at municipal crematoria. We are so frightened of death we want to pretend it doesn't happen. Having children is one of the ways people feel they can lock into immortality. 'Parents live on in the hearts of their children' is a popular refrain. Some of the interviewees expressed sadness and fear because they won't have a child to act as a buffer between them and death. 'The only thing that's on the plus side of having a baby is that there's a part of you that stays when you've gone, and that appeals to me. The idea that there would be a little bit of me that's still here. I'm quite scared of dying, so maybe that's why: I don't like the idea that I'm temporary. It's sad, but it won't swing me the other way into having children,' says Maria, 29.

Another woman has been influenced by eugenics. 'You can't breed good stock from poor,' assets Maud, 75. 'I don't think my genes are worth reproducing: psychopathy goes back in my family to the Renaissance. I'm terribly aggressive and physical violence is there. That's probably why my sister and I used to fight so much. When people say, "Why don't you want children?" I say there's enough fools in the world already.'

Others believe that having a child does not give them access to life eternal. 'I'm spiritual yes, but I don't believe in an afterlife,' says Marie, a journalist. 'I don't believe a child would let me live on and I'm not really frightened by death. I try to live a moral life and to do as much good as I can. I'm trying to improve the world and I think I'm in a better position if I don't have children.' Marie touches on the idea that it is positive deeds in life which continue to flourish after death, something which Sue, 33, also believes: 'Energy doesn't just disappear, it mutates into different forms. I could use my energy to give birth to and raise a child, or I could write a book which changes the way people think, I could fight for justice which would change the way people live. I could save trees in the Amazon which would breathe life into the planet.' Sue is talking about leaving a legacy of love and compassion behind her, a philosophy at the heart of all religions, from the Eastern notion of karma to the biblical assertion 'love is strong as death'.[18] Janet probably has James Lovelock's Gaia theories in mind about the world being one enormous living organism when she says, 'Maybe I won't have my children and grandchildren preserving my memory by crying at my grave, but the roots of every tree and flower grow out of organic rot.'

4

MAKING THE DECISION

How does a woman decide not to have children? There is no one simple answer to this question. The routes that lead to the decision are multifarious and complex; both hugely emotional and social, reflecting the importance of what motherhood means to women, and also what it means to not be a mother. Many of the interviewees found it hard to articulate exactly how they reached their conclusion, probably because it's nonsensical to try and pick out one or two factors as being The Reason. Often, too, firm decisions have not been made: for as many women who have closed the door on the issue by choosing sterilisation, there are those who have kept the door open, have no long-term certainty and are making the decision on a daily, weekly or yearly basis.

'Many times I have thought about the issue and decided not to go ahead, but that doesn't mean I don't address the issue again and again, and I'm sure I will continue doing so for a good few years yet,' says Jo, 39, who has been in a stable relationship for the past fifteen years, although she and her partner keep separate homes. 'On one level I make a decision every time I use contraception; I made a decision nine years ago when I had an abortion; and I make a decision every time I sit down and think about it. However, these decisions are only relevant for the particular time I make them. I have to think about it again when circumstances change. It's easier to say I have never made a decision to have a child.' Jo has a valuable point. Let's invert this chapter's opening question: how does a woman decide to have children?

The idea that having a child actually involves making a decision is a modern one. When thinking about how their parents 'reached the decision' to start a family, most of the interviewees said that it was something their parents entered into automatically, without question. 'It was the "natural step" after marriage,' says Vicky, who comes from a family of three children. 'As Catholics they left it to nature, I suspect,' says Annabelle, also from a family of three. 'It was the thing to do. I doubt they discussed it in detail or analysed their views,' says Terri, who has two sisters. 'I'm not sure there ever was a conscious decision made. They both assumed they would have kids, it was only a matter of when,' says Janet, who has a younger brother. For today's baby-producing generation too, the decision to go ahead and try for children is often a 'non-decision'. Since 1979, the marriage research organisation One Plus One has been following 65 couples through their first years of marriage, and says that a lot of couples start to get sloppy with contraception, putting themselves in the hands of fate. 'They start playing roulette with their contraception, and then express surprise at their pregnancy,' says research officer Fiona McAllister. 'Actually planning a family was a frightening ideal, yet they somehow reached a point when they weren't using contraception all the time.'

The non-decision not to have children

Making a decision is scary, whether it's to have children, or not. There are tremendous losses and gains on both sides and it's a mammoth task to weigh all these up. Some women sit on the fence, effectively making a decision by continually postponing their decision until the menopause arrives and nature makes the final resolution. This could be seen as a positive stance; being always open to change. In the words of 33-year-old Sue, 'I would never say never, so I always have this ambivalence.' Says Tanujah, 'I've made a definite decision for now, but things can be overturned. I have been broody before when I was in a long-term relationship with an Asian man and thought I was pregnant. I got this nice feeling in the pit of my stomach at the thought of our baby. It was a false alarm and I was relieved. I do think about regretting not having children. Sometimes I think that maybe it's an experience that all women should go through. Who's to say how my feelings will change? I'd have to be with the right partner who would be willing to do his share. I also plan to train as a nurse some day, so I don't know how a child would ever fit in.' Emily, 22, nearly faced the possibility of prematurely having her options curtailed when in a dreadful hospital blunder she was mistakenly diagnosed as having cancer of the cervix. 'The doctor warned me that it was possible I might not be able to have children. That made me feel devastated because I thought, what if I change my mind? The fear of never being able to have children was terrible. I kept looking at babies when I was out, thinking I'd blown my chances.' When the mistake was discovered Helen experienced great relief. 'Although I can't see children fitting in with my life, becoming a mother must be a wonderful experience. I'm still young, and there's plenty of time to change my mind. I'm open to that.'

American psychologist Mardy Ireland interviewed a hundred women without children, both through infertility and through choice.[1] She describes women who delay making a decision about childbearing until too late as the 'transitional' women who are living 'in the stream of social change. They want to pursue the social and career possibilities that are now open to women, but they also want, or think they might want, to have a family.' These women often have specific criteria that would have to be fulfilled before embarking on motherhood (financial stability, the right partner). 'Still others are simply living their lives as they unfold, with the idea in mind that "some day" they may have a child.' A decision about motherhood is constantly on hold as other aspects of their lives are more important. Says Ireland:

> The pursuit of education, careers, relationships, and so forth are sometimes choices that represent much more of these women's identities than the part that desires motherhood. Realizing this fact in later life enables them to view childlessness less as a loss and more as a recognition of a different sense of self.

Graphic artist and lesbian Penny, 30, says that she has two visions of her future life. 'In one I've got my own artist's studio, somewhere by the sea. I run local art classes, and spend the rest of my life, with no hassles. The other vision is me with a child, bringing it up with my partner. Being gay, there are bound to be problems as I'll constantly have to justify myself. I like the idea of a busy house, full of children and toys. I don't know which life I want more.'

The constant postponement of making a decision can also be seen as emotional paralysis; the woman constantly living in a state of division with a resulting lack of direction and an enormous drain on her energy: sitting on the fence is hard work. 'I seem to keep making the decision,' says Charlotte, 34. 'I used to think I'd have children when I was 28, then 30. I thought at some point I would feel ready for it and that it was the right thing to do. As I approached 30, which seemed to be quite a turning point when many of my friends started to produce, it dawned on me that maybe this feeling was never going to hit me. I found it quite frightening and depressing. I just have to hope that I can live with the decision I'm making.'

Postponement of motherhood is a growing phenomenon. The average age for first births is now over 27, the highest since 1946, and birth rates have increased most in the 35–39 and 40-plus groups. Women delaying childbirth to establish their careers is one factor creating this trend, but there are others. The high cost of housing is also influential: a report published in 1992 by the Joseph Rowntree Foundation shows that one in nine couples say they put off parenthood because of worries about their mortgage or rent.[2] Somewhere along the line, postponement turns into decision: a child-free woman realises she's quite happy the way she is, maybe she's put off having children because she doesn't really want them that much anyway, and the passing years have brought with them a particular lifestyle that's too good to be disrupted. Many couples also feel that their relationship is complete, and that a child would intrude. Sociologist JeanVeevers identifies four different stages of postponement that take a couple from wanting to not wanting children.[3] First they say they will have children when they have achieved certain goals: buying a new house, travelling around the world, securing promotion at work. Then comes postponement for an indefinite time, where couples become increasingly vague about the issue, saying they'll have children when they 'feel more ready'. When 'more ready' doesn't happen, the couple acknowledge for the first time the possibility that they might not ever have children, that they have the choice to remain child-free, and they start to debate the pros and cons. Finally comes the decision to remain child-free, at which point some couples consider sterilisation.

The problem with constant postponement is the biological clock. A woman has a 75 per cent chance of conceiving in her late thirties but only a one in three chance by her early forties. In recent years this has become a fraught issue. 'When to have your baby' reads the coverline of American feminist magazine *Ms* (note that the assumption is 'when' not 'if').[4] A number of books have also appeared on the subject of late mothering.[5] 'What exactly is the best age to start a family?' asks journalist Deborah Holder in the *Guardian* woman's page in an article *Primagravidas in their prime*, 23 January 1992.'For a woman the pressure starts early. By 30, the family and in-laws are growing nervous: at 35 the ticking of your biological clock is threatening to wake the neighbours and by 40 you are considered past it and left in peace.' Certainly for some women who feel torn about having children, gambling with fertility does not

102

minimise conflicts, it merely delays them until they erupt dramatically at the now-or-never age. According to psychotherapist Estela Welldon,:

> this phenomenon can become difficult to bear for some women who have devoted their lives solely to their careers. They have shown determination at the beginning of their adult lives not to have children in order to advance professionally. Women of this group usually come for therapy in their 30s suffering from increasing anxiety and ambivalence about their long-held conviction of not wanting babies.[6]

It's tough, isn't it? Teasing out the different strands of thought and feeling; trying to get in touch with what we *really* want. 'I feel I didn't really make a conscious decision, I just avoided the issue mostly, but having turned 30 I really had to start thinking about what I wanted out of life. I realised I didn't know, and I still don't know four years later,' explains Debbie, who is married. 'I spend a lot of time feeling I ought to have children and feel very lonely and left out because that is what my generation and peers are doing. I don't meet many people in a similar position.' Two years ago Debbie saw a psychotherapist who asked her to write down all her feelings about children and childbirth. 'I wrote that I didn't want children, but over the next ten sessions he managed to convince me that what I actually wanted most in the world was a baby. I got books out of the library about childbirth, got a Mothercare catalogue, thought up names and how I would decorate the spare room. All this was fine until I actually met some children and the idea didn't seem so attractive. I began to realise what a pushover I was, and how someone had managed to influence me against my better judgement. I realised I would be having a baby largely to please my husband's family.' Maybe Debbie's psychotherapist is right, and what Debbie most wants is a child? Or maybe he is bringing to the therapy his own preconceptions about the rightness of women's role as mother? It's impossible to draw a conclusion, but what can be deduced is that many women feel ambivalent about motherhood, and are now willing to express this.

Siobhan, who is 30, shows less anxiety than Debbie over her indecision. 'I don't expect to have children. I can say that and it feels a natural thing for me; it doesn't feel loaded or regretful,' she says. 'On the other hand it doesn't feel fixed in stone. I might change my mind, that's perfectly possible. There's a small possibility and I don't know what it depends on. I'm not ruling it out.'

Michelle McGrath runs London workshops for women like Siobhan. Entitled 'A Baby or Not?', the three-day workshops address whether a woman *really* wants a baby, or whether it's something she is pressurised into doing. So far, McGrath, who is 38 and has a young son, has run twelve workshops, mostly popular with women in their late thirties who feel their options are fast running out. McGrath says that it is powerful for women to come together to explore the issues, despite the differences between them: some are married, others are single, or living with partners, male or female. 'The essence of the course is knowing what you want,' says McGrath. Much of the workshop centres around fear: fear of missing out if a woman doesn't have children; fear of life not being so good again if she does. McGrath says there are no over-arching right answers, only personal solutions. 'I see the whole thing as a small resource for people to go on from.'

As the child-free option becomes more popular, the likelihood is that courses like 'A Baby or Not?' will become more commonplace as women do battle with the vexatious issues.

Reaching a decision

Finally making a firm decision can involve some relief. 'I felt like a cloud had lifted,' says one woman. Some of the interviewees could recall the precise moment. 'I can remember the exact time and date that we decided not to have children,' says Louise, 34. 'It was a wet spring Bank Holiday in 1981, two and half years before we got married. We had a day out to various tourist attractions where we had seen many families. It struck me then that all the parents and children seemed miserable. The children were constantly moaning, asking for things, or being told off. The parents never spoke to each other unless it was about the children. As one, we turned to each other and said that we really didn't feel that we would want children and have never changed our opinion since.' For Sarah, 31, it happened when she accidentally became pregnant and felt she'd lost control over her life; she subsequently had an abortion. Pregnancy scares similarly brought the decision into focus, as did choices of contraception. Some women who wanted to come off the pill because they had been on it for a number of years, decided to opt for sterilisation; nothing else was considered safe. 'I'm free, completely free,' says Jane, 29, who, having been sterilised a year ago, expresses how reaching a final decision can be a release.

Katy, 23, and her husband called on their Baptist faith to help them, praying for guidance with a Christian fellowship group. 'We tried to find biblical support for our decision but there isn't a lot,' explains Katy. 'The earth is overpopulated now, so a lot of it doesn't apply as it did to Adam and Eve. We are on a two-year course which aims to develop our Christian disciplines like Bible-reading and prayer. One of the things we were studying at the time was how to make decisions. It was suggested we find counsel with other Christians, find biblical support and a sense of peace. With biblical support there wasn't a lot that applied, so it fell down to the other two. All the other people in our home group felt it was right for us, or certainly not wrong for us, to decide not to have children. We also felt really at peace about the decision. When we sent off the request for the vasectomy we got it back so quick (within two weeks) we really had a panic prayer time to see if it was right. Obviously we didn't want to go through it if God wanted us to have children in the future. Even though we had such a sense of peace about it we held in our hearts that even if it wasn't right God would manage not to make the operation work. I know sometimes the vasectomy can reverse itself.'

Many women said that they'd reached a decision not to have children at a young age. For Julia, 32, the die was cast extremely young. 'I have never been able to visualise myself as a wife and mother. Even as a little girl I wasn't interested in playing "weddings", "bathing baby", etc. I knew by the age of 12 that I didn't want to have children. Likewise with Angie, for whom the murmurs started at a tender age. 'I can remember the first time I thought about it was when I was at school and we found out how babies were made. I thought, I don't want to have a baby. I felt really uncomfortable about the whole idea.' Says Linda, 'There was never, ever any time when I wanted them. At about eight or nine I can remember asking my father what you do if you got married and your husband wanted children and you didn't.'

For Sue, 33, lack of interest in family life surfaced in her teens: 'I knew as a teenager that I didn't want to get married. When I was 14 I went to see a palmist on Brighton pier, and she said, "You'll be married by the time you're 21 and you'll have two children, and a nurse would be a good profession for you." I heard all this and it struck terror into my heart. For months afterwards I was in a terrible state: somehow I thought this would happen to me without my wanting it to. How dreadful it would be.'

Influential people

The influence of two people looms especially large when making the decision not to have children: the woman's partner, and her mother. Women in stable relationships made the decision together with their partner, and his views on the matter were crucial. The influence of the woman's mother was more subtle and indirect, but nevertheless very powerful, and will be fully explored in the next section. More remote figures had sometimes made an impact. Several of the interviewees mentioned having met a woman without children who was living her life very positively.

For Karen it was her music teacher, whom she met in her teens. She was married and used to talk openly about her enjoyment of life without children. I found this a philosophy I could identify with, and we remain friends to this day.' Similarly when Ilona was in her teens she met someone who planted the idea that a woman didn't have to have children to lead a full life. 'When I was a patient in hospital at 15, a married child-free nurse used to talk to me about her life. She was very happy and was a caring and fulfilled person. To me she had everything she needed and I realised one didn't have to conform. Decisions are personal things.' Penny looks around at other older lesbians, and says that there is no shortage of role models for her: 'I can think of one couple in particular who always seem happy. They're both in their late forties and have never been hit by longings to give birth or foster children.' Josephine, 63, remembers her youth and an aunt who worked as a fashion buyer in a large London store. At the time it was unusual for a woman to have such a dynamic career, and Josephine was greatly impressed. 'I wanted to be like her. She was single, and didn't get married till in her fifties. I used to have tea with her on Saturday afternoons when I moved to London. She was a glamour figure to me. She was smartly dressed and had an important job and seemed very sophisticated. She had a little stock of drink in her flat and that was very sophisticated.' Helen admired the relationship of a child-free couple she met a couple of years ago, who were in their forties, 'but still in love and into having a good time together'.

Alternatively, women who had become mothers and seemed to be struggling with the role had a negative impact. 'I feel my decision had a lot to do with my sister coming to stay at my parents' house with her three boys,' says Debbie. 'Until then I had thought kids were OK but after a week or so of three boys under six I realised what hard work they were. Also I saw the effect having children had on my sister financially and intellectually. She had no interests of her own and her entire conversation revolved around children. Despite bringing up the three boys which she had felt both of them wanted, her husband left her for one of her friends, so their children didn't keep them together and she was left quite badly off.' Sally too cites unhappy parents as influential: 'Some of the first people I knew of around my age to have children had a fairly disastrous time and two of the couples involved are now divorced.'

My mother, myself?

'My mother was always a role model for how *not* to lead your life,' says Jo. Such sentiments were very common among the women I interviewed. The past thirty years have seen tumultuous changes in the role of women. Never before in history has the young woman been so set apart from her mother: in attitude, expectations and opportunity. It is clear from many of the interviews that young women look back at their mothers' lives as if across a ravine. Mother represents the past, the old way of doing things; she's a dinosaur to be pitied, despised, feared and patronised as well as loved. All these feelings were expressed by the interviewees, and with such forcefulness that it quickly became apparent that whoever she was, mother was very *significant*. When asked, 'Who has been the most important person to you when making the decision to remain child-free?' some women said: my mother.

How do we imagine what it might be like to become a mother? Undoubtedly our primary source of knowledge about motherhood comes from our own mothers. Did my mum enjoy being a mother? Was it something that was forced upon her? Did she have to give up a career to look

109

after her family? Was being at home with small children a lonely, frustrating experience? Did children trap her in an unhappy marriage? All these questions are very pertinent for many of the child-free women who assimilated their mothers' lives over the years and concluded that mother-hood was not necessarily the gateway through which we must pass in order to become *whole* women. 'My mother would be very upset if she knew how I feel,' says Georgina, 32. 'She fell into the stereotypical mould and felt that we were her life: if we were happy, she was happy. She was very satisfied as she saw it as her goal in life to have kids. It had an effect on me, seeing my mother always being short of money and having to go to my father for anything she wanted. Also she was always tired and worried about us all the time. I feel that women ignore themselves in favour of their children. Mum would go without food to feed us, or if she was ill she would leave it so long before going to the GP: if we were ill we went straight away.'

In America between 1982 and 1988, cultural historian Shere Hite surveyed 874 women and girls, asking them open questions about their mothers. A staggering 83 per cent said they had a terrific fear of being like their mothers, and responses were as dramatic as: 'If I thought I was like her, I'd put a gun to my head.' 'What *is* this fear we have of "being like our mothers?" ,' asks Shere Hite. 'Is it fear of being second-class, not important, not counting? of developing subservient behaviours? or is it fear of being considered "unattractive" and "old" ?'[7] In *Of Woman Born*,[8] Adrienne Rich informs us that there's even a word for this phenomenon: matrophobia means, not fear of one's own mother or of becoming a mother, but fear of becoming one's own mother. 'I saw how much my mother gave to us in terms of emotion. I feel she almost gave too much of herself,' explains Julia, 'though she once said to me that she would not have been heartbroken if she couldn't have had children, and was never all over other people's children. I learnt from this that there is more to life than marrying and having children.'

It is only now that women are not immediately expected to abandon their careers to have children. The mothers of all the women I interviewed had little option but to give up their paid jobs when they started a family. Many of my interviewees saw this as a terrible waste of their mothers' talents. 'It was so unfair,' says one; 'I feel sorry for her,' says another. Marnie, 31, believes that her mother would have been a much more interesting person if she'd kept her career as an occupational therapist: 'I don't think my dad wanted her to work after she gave birth to my older brother. She says she enjoyed being a mother, but I'm not sure that she did, really. She doesn't know what's going on in the world, doesn't go out, hasn't got any friends. She spends too long thinking about my brother who has schizophrenia. It's a shame; she had such a good job at a time when most women didn't work.' Says Katrin: 'My mother was more of a career woman, she would have liked a good career. She was at university and she had to give up her studies because she was pregnant with me.'

The isolated mother at home with small screaming children and only the television for company is now a familiar image. In the 1950s the image of women's domestic life was idealised as a result of the decline of feminism between 1930 and 1950; but by the 1960s a new picture emerged, quite different from the sentimental illustrations of beaming mothers in Bird's Custard and Horlicks advertisements. In what is now a classic study, *The Captive Wife*,[9] sociologist Hannah Gavron interviewed 96 mothers with small children in 1966, the women who are now the mothers to daughters, who, like many of my interviewees, are in their early thirties. Gavron concluded that 'The advent of children brings with it isolation and insecurity . . . it is also a time which involves a great loss of confidence to many a young woman.' She noted that for many women the nuclear family was her only source of contact, and that their main contact with the outside world was the television set. Middle-class women fared slightly better than working-class, who tended to be even more inward looking. For example, 69 per cent of the middle-class women had had some sort of contact with their neighbours, as opposed to only 29 per cent of the working-class sample. Many of my interviewees vividly remember their mothers' exile. 'She was trapped at home with the kids and the only person she'd see for days on end was my dad,' says Penny. Tanujah says that Asian women of her mother's generation are even more restricted. 'Part of the Asian culture is that men control the women. My elder brother won't let my mother out. He's a bit of a tyrant and she has to ask his permission to go out.'

Many of the women also see that having children meant that their mothers were trapped in unhappy marriages. Says 75-year-old Maud, 'My mother was a very intelligent woman and my father was a clever man, but they were totally incompatible, and I think their marriage must have been hell. In those days if you were poor you couldn't afford to part, so she had to put up with it. But she told me once, "For God's sake don't have any children; you'll just stay in the gutter." If she hadn't had my sister and me, being intelligent she would have gone out and trained to do something, but my father wouldn't let her work. He was in the Navy, then he became a signalman for London Transport. My mother was a marvellous cook and she could do the most beautiful needlework.' Says Sally, 32: 'My mother often threatened to walk out the door and never come back, but she didn't because of us. Once we all grew up and left home my parents didn't seem to have anything in common. They nearly separated in their seventies.'

The differences that exist between mothers and daughters bring with them difficult, painful feelings on both sides. While some mothers will their daughters to struggle for the independence that was so elusive in their lives, sadly others feel resentment about their daughters' increased opportunities. A mother may feel rejected as her daughter chooses a very different life, conveying the message that mum is shallow, trivial and somehow inferior. Says Sue: 'My mother was furious when I broke up with my long-term boyfriend Peter. She said, "Well, there were plenty of times when I was fed up with your father, but I didn't leave him. Where could I have gone? What could I have done?" I thought, well, that's not my position: I can go somewhere else, and do something else. I think that a lot of the resentment that comes from your parents about not supplying them with grandchildren is to do with the opportunities which weren't available to them. The opportunities that were open to my mother weren't very great, in the sense that she wasn't a very intelligent woman or educated. Quite typically of that period, she was ambitious through my father. He was in management for the Electricity Board, and when he reached a certain level wouldn't take any more promotion because he didn't

113

want the hassles. I think secretly my mother was very bitter about this because her position would have been enhanced.

'She never really encouraged my academic achievements. When I said I wanted to go to university I can remember her being quite angry about it, saying, "Nonsense, what is the point of going to university, you'll just get married and it will be a waste of time. You might as well get a job as a secretary, get married and then it will all be fine." It was suggested to me by a friend that my mother was quite unhappy in her marriage, and she won't be happy until she sees me in the same situation: I thought that was quite true. I think it's been very destructive: I hate my mother. Her hidden agenda is that she would like me to be something very stable and contained that doesn't surpass her ideas of what I should be: surely if I become something else it reflects rather badly on her, and the opportunities she never took up.'

A daughter comparing her life with her mother's may feel guilt and sadness for the woman who sacrificed so much to raise her. 'I look at myself, travelling, working, doing further education, all the things mum wanted to do but never could because she was stuck at home with babies and a mortgage,' says Jane, 29. 'When I tell my mother I don't want children, I feel that what I'm really saying is the role she put so much of her life into is worthless to me, and that I think so little of her efforts as a mother that I don't want to repeat the cycle. Feeling this guilt was so unexpected and difficult to deal with because it's an emotional thing, and rational arguments don't work with it.'

Since the 1970s there has been much interest in the mother/daughter relationship and a number of popular books have been published on the subject.[10] It's often

114

easier to respond negatively to our mother than to see beyond the socioeconomic forces that shape her. In America, professor of psychology Karen G. Howe teaches a psychology of women course, in which she encourages students to write their mothers' biographies. They are asked to interview their mothers about their lives as children, adolescents and young women before they became mothers. I suspect that if we were to do this exercise, many of us would be meeting our mothers for the very first time; getting to know them as women in their own right and not just in the role which relates to us. Howe finds that students acquire new perceptions of their mothers as a product of their social and family environments, and as a result often feel much less anger towards them. Similar results are achieved in psychotherapy with the use of 'genogram': a way of mapping out your parents' lives and the influential social factors.

Such techniques mark the beginnings of bridge-building across generations. It is not only between mothers and daughters that bridges need to be built, but also between women of the same generation who make different choices about parenthood. The child-free women often say that their lifestyle is viewed by women with children as an attack on them: the issue evokes strong feelings. Sometimes they feel that mothers are jealous of the child-free. 'A lot of my friends say that if they had their time over again they would make the same decision as me. They love their children dearly but just feel restricted by them. In a way they feel a little jealous of me, and a couple of my friends have actually said as much,' says Georgina. Others said that friends with children are hostile or 'persistently choose not to hear what I'm saying'. In writing this book I have felt awkward when explaining its subject to friends who are mothers. Women are very sensitive to the differences between them, but learning how to celebrate and honour the variation is a challenge that we cannot ignore.

Influence of feminism

Feminism has played a momentous part in a child-free woman's decision-making. If it had not been for the feminist movement women would not have the reliable contraception and safe abortion which enables them to control their fertility, nor would they have access to the careers which many find so satisfying and see as a creative alternative to motherhood. While a couple of the interviewees did not feel that feminism had influenced their lives, others were very positive.

Feminist thinking has contributed enormously to the debate about motherhood during the past thirty years. It has exposed its emotional pains and pleasures; examined motherhood as a patriarchal institution; discussed the ethics of controlling fertility in an overpopulated world; looked at the experience of infertile women and those who choose not to become mothers; and investigated the tensions between mothering and paid employment. In an article in *Feminist Review*[11] Ann Snitow surveys past American writing on feminism and motherhood and comes up with a 'time-line' of writing, listing over 150 seminal books and articles spanning the years 1963–90.

Here's what some of the interviewees had to say:

I read Simone de Beauvoir when I was 15 and there's a whole thing about mothers and motherhood and so on. I read it and realised I was the second sex, and I didn't want to be the second sex. It totally changed my vision of my life. (Marie, 44)

I read two books in my early twenties that really made me think, *The Baby Trap* [Ellen Peck] and *Mother's Day is Over* [Shirley Radl]. (Julia, 32) [Both these books, published in the early 1970s, highlighted the drudgery that comes with the institution of motherhood and validated the option of a child-free lifestyle.]

It has given me the permission to do many things I felt guilty about in earlier life. (Jo, 39)

It's given me the confidence to pursue a career and to fight to keep my identity and to make my own decisions. (Liz, 40)

I think it's paved the way for me to develop a real career and choose not to have children. I believe in equal rights and equal opportunities and think it's important that women lead their lives to the full and do what they find satisfying. If feminism can support that, it's doing a good job. (Amelia, 22)

It has taught me to ask questions, explore alternatives and look at things and situations from new angles, rather than just going along with the flow and doing what was expected of me. More then anything else it was my experience of and readings in feminism that showed me it was all right to be different from the majority, not to want the same things out of life that most other people did, and that I had a right to my own feelings and beliefs even if they conflicted with other people's. (Penny, 30)

117

Menopause

If a woman is still in some doubt about whether or not to have children, somewhere between the age of 48 to 53 nature finally makes up its mind for her. Her periods will become erratic and the blood-flow lighter or heavier, or they may just suddenly stop altogether. This is the menopause: the time when the ovaries stop producing a monthly ovum and cease the secretion of the cyclic supply of oestrogen. There will also be a decline in the production of the hormone progesterone. Women may experience hot flushes as the body adjusts to its new hormonal balance, and a decrease in vaginal moisture, known as vaginal atrophy. Why do women have a menopause? Men remain fertile throughout their lives. Everything in nature is said to have its purpose, and the menopause ensures that a woman does not go through the hazards of giving birth late in life. It also protects children against being born to mothers who will not live long enough to raise them.

After the menopause life will never quite be the same again, and coming to terms with this dramatic change can involve physical, emotional and spiritual adjustment. The terrain of menopause is demanding, and some women have a more difficult time than others. In the words of Germaine Greer in *The Change*,[12] it is lamentable not to experience anything significant about the menopause because 'the goal of life is not to feel nothing'. Greer describes it poetically:

At menopause as never before a woman comes face to face with her own mortality. A part of her is dying. If she has been encouraged all her life to think of her reproductive faculty as her most important

118

contribution, the death of her ovaries will afflict her deeply. Nothing she can do will bring her ovaries back to life. The grief of menopause affects every woman consciously or otherwise. The feeling that one's day has passed its noon and the shadows are lengthening, that summer is long gone and the days are growing ever shorter and bleaker, is a just one and should be respected.

For a child-free woman who harbours some regrets about not experiencing motherhood the menopause may be a time when she painfully takes stock of what she has achieved in her life and what she has yet to achieve. 'When the menopause looms you tend to start thinking about it. You're bound to have some regret,' says Marion, 41, a journalist. 'Having children is the thing that's supposed to be the one major achievement for a woman, some people say it's their whole reason for being, to produce. I do sometimes think, God, there's no continuity here. If I really let myself think about it I could get quite wound up. Whatever the reason it hasn't happened and wasn't meant to happen: it wasn't right for you. One day I might produce something I'm really proud of out of the word processor and I'll think that's what I was here for.'

The menopause is a relatively modern phenomenon. At the time of the Roman Empire the average life span of a woman was a fleeting 23 years, and even by the Victorian era it was only 45 years (the average being lowered by disease and death in childbirth). Today 50 per cent of women in developed countries reach the age of 75, and spend a third of their lives without the capacity to bear children. These unreproductive years have contributed to our adjustment in thinking about the meanings of a woman's life: to seeing childbearing as just one possible aspect of it, rather than its driving purpose. The Boston Women's Health Collective, writing in *Our Bodies Ourselves*,[13] say that 'as women start to value themselves as more than baby machines, as we increasingly view middle age as a welcome time offering new freedom and we make selective use of various treatments to minimize any menopausal discomforts, the menopause can be a positive experience.'

In recent years, cracks have appeared in the new positive stance to life beyond maternity. Some medical experts have pioneered controversial techniques which try to trick nature into delaying the menopause and make mothers out of women who are as old as 62. There are two areas of medical exploration: delaying menopause by removing the ovary of a woman while young, putting it on ice, and then reintroducing it to her body some years later. As the undisturbed ovary dies, the defrosted one takes over, artificially postponing menopause. *In vitro* fertilisation (IVF) is the other area of research: first treating a post-menopausal woman with hormones, then implanting a fertilised donor egg and introducing more hormones into her body to sustain its gestation. For many couples who suffer fertility problems and desperately want children, new fertility treatments like IVF have been miraculous. There are critics, however. 'Through in vitro fertilisation, women have become seen as body parts: eggs, ovaries, wombs, sometimes for rent and often for use by others,' argues Dr Robyn Rowland, author of *Living Laboratories: Women and Reproductive Technology*.[14]

Shouldn't the post-menopausal years be a season of liberation from the tensions of reproduction? It seems that no price is too high in order to promote a woman's role as childbearer, and that many women still view maternity as the focal point of existence. While in some quarters the energies of medical technology are locked in battle with the inevitable, many women are able to greet the ageing process rather than run away from it. For those interviewees who felt very certain that they didn't want children, the menopause meant release and relaxation. Says 69-year-old Lucy, 'I wasn't bothered that I would no longer be able to have children. I looked forward to it in a way. It was a relief, no more worry.' For other women the issues of reproductive capacity played little part in the experience. 'I didn't think about it in terms of childbearing. There were very heavy periods, and I thought this is probably it, then I stopped having periods, and I thought how nice it was not to have them,' says Josephine, 63.

Turning points in our lives are vital, giving us direction, new energies and a deeper understanding of ourselves. Says Greer, after the stress of the first encounter with 'the change' 'the ageing woman realize(s) that autumn can be long, golden, milder and warmer than summer, and is the most productive season of the year'.

Ageing

While everyone is a potential victim of loneliness, elderly people are especially vulnerable. *The Health of the Nation*, a publication by the Department of Health, reads: 'The prevalence of most types of mental illness is just as high amongst elderly people as in the population as a whole. However, depression, suicide and dementia are more common and the problems associated with bereavement and isolation increase.'

It's fairly easy to measure social isolation: it's impossible to count how many people someone sees each week, how often they speak to someone on the phone, receive letters, and so on. Loneliness, however, is an emotional issue and harder to quantify. It's a huge fear for many people, and an anxiety expressed by the interviewees. 'Loneliness in old age is my greatest fear,' says Helen, 26. Despite the breakdown of extended family structures, there are still expectations that our children and grandchildren will protect us from the feelings of loneliness that can come with ageing. Janette, 30, projects the fear at its worst: 'I don't have any family left, I'm the last one. I'm all on my own in some little room hunched up in blankets.' Maybe I should have a child so at least I have got somebody for when I'm older, someone to look after me,' says Tanujah. She points out that within Asian culture there are strong family obligations to care for the elderly. 'My 80-year-old gran lives with my uncle, and comes to stay with us when he goes on holiday.'

In *Loneliness How to Overcome It*,[15] psychologist Peter Honey explains that there are two types of loneliness: external, which is caused by a situation, and internal which is brought about by thoughts, beliefs and attitudes. 'Being on a desert island would be an example of external loneliness,' says Honey, 'but the effect of being alone in a hostile world can be created, say, following a bereavement or the break-up of a relationship. People who suffer the most intense loneliness at such a time are those who are, to a great extent, dependent on others for the way they feel. True loneliness is created by both internal and external causes.'

It is easy to make assumptions that the child-free who are living alone in later years will be particularly lonely, but is this really true? There's much to be said for the saying that you can be lonely in a crowd. Families are often thought to be an insurance policy against loneliness in old age, yet ironically, according to one study, many elderly people who live with their adult children feel lonely.[16] Another study points out: 'We tend to think of widows, childless people and the never-married . . . as at risk. In fact, the never-married tend to be less vulnerable, having well developed strategies for establishing and maintaining social contacts.'[17]

Several of the interviewees demonstrated their determination to socialise and make new contacts should they feel lonely. 'I would just get out there and do something: go walking or join a club, whatever. There's no way I would sit and feel sorry for myself. People need people, but you don't necessarily have to have kids,' says Phillippa, 40. 'There are plenty of lonely people who have children. They're no guarantee of company. If I'm alone I'll join a club, or get a dog or cat,' says Sally, 32. Marie, who is divorced, says: 'You make more friends when you are alone.'

Having family around may have an impact on whether we feel lonely, but it might not be the most important factor. In a recent report on loneliness psychologist David Weeks estimates that isolation, characterised by extremely infrequent contacts with other people, affects about one in ten elderly people.[18] He says:

Most at risk are those who retired from humbler, more poorly paid positions in employment, divorced people and widowers. The absence of children and relatives in the immediate area, the lack of professional ties and, above all, a psychological disposition to shyness and

123

introversion, are the main underlying causes of this risk group.

In the same report social anthropologist Dorothy Jerrome stresses the importance of friends rather than family. 'It is often thought that loneliness among widows might be reduced by visits from children. But in fact such visits make little impact on loneliness and very old widows living with adult children are frequently among the most lonely.' She concludes that 'friendship is more important than family in reducing loneliness in old age'.

Several of the interviewees would agree with Jerrome that family relationships are often disappointing, and that friendships can be more satisfying. Says Karen, 'I visit a few elderly people, not family, occasionally, and it's fascinating to observe that the widows clearly divide into mothers who constantly complain about how much they are not seeing their offspring, obviously a great source of pain for these ladies: and then one lady who has never had children and consequently doesn't expect this attention from anyone, and furthermore she sustains a lifelong circle of friends.' Marnie looks critically at the relationship she has with her own parents: 'My parents are old and I only see them two or three times a year.' Miriam used to work in a hospital and thinks of the elderly patients she came into contact with: 'I don't think you can say I'm going to have children to make sure there's somebody to look after me when I'm old: it won't work like that. Often they've gone to Australia, can't be bothered, or aren't interested. I've met old ladies in geriatric wards at work who were dumped by the families they devoted their lives to. They say things to you on the wards, "I wish I could get out of here but my daughter won't have me", things like that.'

Lucy, who is 69, cared for her mother until she died at the age of 96, an experience which she says exhausted her, but that she was glad to be able to do. Interestingly it has left her feeling uncomfortable with the idea of family obligation. 'My sympathies tend to be with the offspring leading their own lives. Parents shouldn't expect too much. The fact I haven't got children is in a way a relief. If I was old and dependent on someone they might feel that they've got a duty. They'd have to leave their own lives to look after me. It would be nice to have a young person who would come and visit me in the home and make sure I was all right, but I wouldn't want them to give up their lives. It's possible that a niece or nephew would check up on me once a year or something.'

Lucy lives on her own and has few close relatives. She is, however, someone who has a lot of friends. She is involved in adult education, goes to a dance group, and is very active in her local church. At Christmas she works for a charity helping the homeless. While I was interviewing her she received several phone calls from friends, and is obviously much cared for within her community.

In contrast, Maud, 75, moved from London to Devon when she retired. She too lives alone. Her life does seem isolated: she has little contact with her closest relative, her sister, and has no friends in Devon because she is newly settled. There is of course a distinction between being alone and being lonely. Some people enjoy their own company, lots of it, and are not reliant on others for how they feel. Being alone can mean finding peace. 'I could have people around me, but I don't want them,' Maud says. 'I go to classes, I'm a member of the National Trust,

Greenpeace and the Green Party. There's a local National Trust and all through the year there are visits to places. Also I belong to the twinning association which means I go to France every year. I haven't got people around me I'm close to. I could be living on Mars. Sometimes it worries me, but then on the other hand . . . I enjoy my own company. I get asked out at Christmas but won't go. I stay at home with a nice bottle of wine, I have my videos and music and all the books I want. I'm not lonely.'

Being lonely in old age is a worry for all of us, with or without children, and is partly due to the fact that we live in a culture which undervalues its elderly. Loneliness is built into the structure of our society too: our housing stock is based on self-contained family units, and public transport can be difficult. The British are also terribly concerned about privacy, often to the extent of barricading themselves from each other. When making the decision to remain child-free, fears of future loneliness can be powerful, but need to be rationalised. Says Marion, 'You obviously start to think about your old age, but there are no guarantees. Each child does not arrive with a certificate saying "I guarantee when my mum is old I'll be there". I like to think I'll still have friendships that will see me through. If I'm a lonely and embittered old woman, so be it. What could I have done? Had a kid because I thought I'd be a lonely old woman? And then what? The kid grows up hating you, thinking you're not like other people's mums. There are no guarantees in this world.'

Any regrets?

It was rare for an interviewee to have no regrets at all about not being a mother. There were a few who

126

vehemently declared 'nothing at all' when asked what they feel they miss out on, but for the most part there was a sense that raising children could be joyous, loving and creative, and that child-free women lose as well as gain. Having children provides us with tremendous opportunities to both give and receive love, and there were fears that a child-free woman might somehow be cast adrift because she does not have that solid rooted love that often comes in family relationships. 'I will not have the chance to have another relationship with someone of the type that I have with my mother and father,' says Amelia. 'I'll miss the undiscerning "I love you, mummy" devotion given by a small child,' says Sarah. Other women talked about missing out on children's cuddles and kisses. However, many who were in extremely loving relationships felt that this was love enough for anyone. 'I asked a friend of mine, a mother, what she felt I was missing out on. She answered "complete and utter love". Well, I feel well loved by my husband and family so don't feel I'm missing that,' says Karen.

There were also those who expressed cynicism about family life. 'I suppose you could say I'll miss out, but what is family life nowadays? People in Britain aren't particularly family orientated,' says Elizabeth. 'My friends say, "You'll have no one to visit you at Christmas." I say, "Yeah, you're going home for Christmas, are you looking forward to it?" They say, "No." Well, what makes you think your children are going to be delighted to be with you at Christmas? "Well, because we hope we'll be different and do it better, and our children will love us." OK, how many people do you know who have a really good relationship with their parents? Not many. Good luck,' says Sue.

Some women had fantasised about what sex a child of theirs might have been, and what it would have looked like. One woman had gone one stage further and said she felt sad that she would never have grandchildren. Janet, 29, says that 'the sole regret I think I might have one day is that I'll never have an adult relationship with a grown son or daughter. I think I would like to know a child of mine as an adult, to have a relationship of equals with him or her.'

Despite sometimes wistful thoughts about children that might never be, for the most part the interviewees were unsentimental and rational about their decision. 'There's a very small part of me which thinks you're missing something here, and then I think thousands of women could be decoyed into motherhood by thinking that they're missing something, and nobody speaks about how they regret motherhood,' says Sue. Jo too thoughtfully balances her anxieties about the child-free option with regrets that might have come with motherhood: 'I do worry that I will regret it, but I also worry that if I had had a child I would regret that too. I think regretting the first option is not so devastating as regretting the second.' Says Julia, 'I'm quite sure that for every child-free woman who later regrets her decision, there are literally hundreds of mothers who rue the day they got pregnant.'

Another way that these woman have come to terms with their regrets is by placing childbearing in the larger context of life experiences and putting it into some perspective. Says 63-year-old Josephine, 'Once or twice with friends' children I've thought, oh I've missed that experience haven't I? But it's never meant more to me than any other experience one's missed. Life is full of experiences one hasn't had. You can't have all the experiences in the world. It was a decision that was right for me, and it's fine. Whatever you do in life you miss the alternative. You have to focus on what you're doing and why you're doing it, and not what you're not doing, because you're always not doing something. It's futile to think about what you're not doing: I'm not climbing Everest, I'm not going in a hot-air balloon over India and all sorts of other delightful things. Nobody does everything.'

There is also a sense that harbouring regrets is futile and unproductive: 'I think it's inevitable that I'll wonder about the path not taken, whether I would have been happy with children, and how different my life would have been,' says Janet. 'I think particularly in times of stress it will be easy to wonder whether I made the wrong decision, and whether a child might not have made that vital difference. But I can also see how that might be true of many other choices and turning points in my life, and I want to make the best of whatever future I choose for myself, not waste it regretting what can't be changed.'

5

CONTRACEPTION CHOICES AND ABORTION

IT IS only in relatively modern times that we have been able to control our fertility with any degree of reliability. In the past not having children meant not having sex, or at least investing a lot of hope in the power of crossed fingers and prayer. The desire to control fertility is not a new phenomenon: contraception dates back much further than the hundred-odd years since the beginning of family planning development and the opening of the first 'birth control' clinic in 1921. Women have long tried to limit the number of children born, from the use of magic rituals and potions onwards, often to little effect.

Some of the terrible extremes to which women have gone in order to prevent pregnancy illustrate our determination to control fertility. As late as 1883 women are thought to have used carbolic acid as a douche, and half-poisoned themselves with herbal concoctions in the hope of miscarrying. Until the legalisation of abortion in

Britain in 1967 knitting needles, razors and douches were a common last resort for desperate women. There were probably many of these as, in the first days of family planning, services were available only for married women. No one knows how many deaths are attributable to back-street abortions; their illegality prevented some doctors from reporting associated deaths. However, it is estimated that over 3 million abortions have taken place in the UK since the 1967 Abortion Act. This works out at one abortion every three minutes. Writing in France in 1949, before abortion was legalised, Simone de Beauvoir said that

> the pregnant woman appeals to a woman friend, or operates on herself. These non-professional surgeons are often incompetent; they are prone to cause perforation by probe or knitting needle. A doctor told me of an ignorant cook who, in the attempt to inject vinegar into the uterus, injected it into the bladder, which was atrociously painful.[1]

Josephine, 63, a retired teacher, remembers her own difficulties in finding a backstreet abortionist as a young married woman. She used a contraceptive cap, but in 1955, aged 25, she became pregnant. Neither she nor her husband felt that they wanted a child at this stage of their lives, and Josephine was already questioning whether she ever would want one. 'I suspected that I didn't ever want children, but at the forefront of my mind was how to get rid of this one. I didn't dither about whether to have an abortion or not, the only problem was how to find one. One asked around: do you know anybody? My husband found someone through a colleague at work, a retired nurse. One phoned up and it was all assumed names and, you know, a friend of mine is in trouble and I've heard you might be able to help. She was very cagey and wanted to know where we'd got her name. One fixed up an appointment on the telephone, then went and had a talk with her. She sussed you out, I suppose: that you weren't an informer or undercover police spy. I can't remember how much it cost, but it was a considerable sum of money: probably a month's salary or more. It was done at her home. She used a kind of syringe and douched me with soapy water that precipitated labour. I was terrified. I was sent off home, where I miscarried.' All of the women I interviewed have led or lead sexually active lives, with the exception of Julia, a 32-year-old foundry worker. Her lack of self-esteem possibly fuels her negativity about relationships. 'I've never had or wanted to have a boyfriend,' she says, 'which is probably a good thing as no one has ever shown the least bit of romantic interest in me. If I had been brought up in a very religious Catholic family I would quite probably have become a nun.' Most of the women expressed satisfaction with their chosen methods of contraception, although fifteen of the fifty had had an abortion at some stage.

Abortion: the debate

Debates on the rights and wrongs of abortion illuminate important ideas about what it means to be a woman. When a woman demands an abortion, she is saying: I do not want to become a mother (to another child, or at this present time). Could it be that the debate confronts head-on the belief that this is her highest accolade – her ultimate achievement and function? This view was recently supported by the rapturous response in Italy to the death of a woman who refused cancer treatment which she feared would damage her unborn baby. Carla Levati Ardenghi refused an abortion which would have enabled her to undergo potentially life-saving chemotherapy, a decision supported by her 28-year-old husband. She subsequently died in January 1993 after prematurely giving birth to a baby boy by Caesarean section. The baby also died ten days later. The husband now has to bring up their first child, a 10-year-old boy, single-handedly. Carla Levati Ardenghi immediately became a national heroine. 'She defeated death and affirmed the idea of maternity as immortality,' proclaimed the Italian newspaper, *La Stampa*. Although her choice can be seen as noble and courageous, it has been seized upon by Catholic groups in an attempt to promote the anti-abortionist cause. A few weeks before Ardenghi's death, the Roman Catholic Church announced that Gianni Beretta, a women who died in 1962 in almost identical circumstances, is to be beatified. The most profound, saintly meaning ascribed to these lives is clear: women should be mothers no matter what the cost.

Abortion: the experience

'I would have used everything, even a knitting needle. When I had the abortion I never felt any remorse: I was just so bloody grateful.' (Sue, 33)

Very few of the interviewees have moral objections to early abortion. Like Sue, they feel thankful and relieved that they have the right to choose whether to continue with a pregnancy. Sue was at university when she discovered she was pregnant: 'I fell in an amazing way for this black guy who was much older than me. He was very sophisticated and exciting. When I found out I was pregnant I was in a dreadful panic. I was abroad for the summer holidays working in Germany. I phoned this guy up but he wouldn't take my calls: he literally abandoned me. I was so stubborn I wouldn't go home immediately and have the abortion: I didn't want it to interfere with my plans for the summer. What did I feel like being pregnant? I did have sideways glances at these babies on the street, particularly the mixed-race ones, and thought: it could be something like that. But mostly I thought: what will I do with a kid? It seemed nothing to do with me; I won't be able to relate to it. When I eventually got back home I was four months pregnant: I looked pregnant; my friends even said I stood like a pregnant woman. I went to see the doctor at college and was in tears. Uppermost in my mind was that I would ruin my life: I would have to do some sort of job to support this kid and all my plans would go adrift.'

An accidental pregnancy brings feelings about motherhood into sharp focus. A decision has to be made very quickly: motherhood, adoption or abortion? There is no way out, this is an issue which cannot be avoided. It's time when a woman has to honestly confront her thoughts and feelings about maternity: this is especially difficult for the woman who has avoided making a conscious decision about motherhood but has perpetually delayed childbirth.

First reactions to pregnancy include disbelief, panic, numbness, sometimes joy, 'My husband and I were both a bit proud that things worked and we were able to conceive,' says Janette. Then comes the agony of making a decision: for most women an abortion is more than just a medical procedure; it is a painful experience that may soon be overcome, or may reverberate years later.

134

Any empirical research on the psychological impact of terminations soon becomes embroiled in the politicisation of abortion. Research does not take place in a vacuum: it is impossible to escape the moral and ethical debates that surround abortion. There is a reluctance to call attention to the negative consequences for fear of providing support to anti-abortion groups; likewise research into abortion as a positive choice for women is difficult, in danger of being interpreted as immoral. Consequently there has been little research on the subject, and what exists is controversial and often negative.

Some professionals identify a condition called 'post-abortion syndrome': in 1987 a survey by the anti-abortion voluntary organisation LIFE showed that 40 per cent of women suffer emotionally after abortion. Statistics vary wildly: in that same year in America, a study suggested that 65 per cent of women who'd had an abortion and were questioned had thought of suicide, and 31 per cent had attempted it. Another American study concluded that 19 per cent of women suffer pathological disorders within three to five years of an abortion; another study put the figure suffering from post-abortion syndrome at 10–50 per cent. The Society for the Protection of the Unborn Child runs British Victims of Abortion, a counselling organisation for women believed to be suffering from 'post-abortion syndrome'. One of its counsellors explains:

> It's like a grieving procedure, grieving for the death of their baby. When you go to a clinic you're dealing with a foetus, but we say it was a baby, and now it's dead. Women can't understand why they're feeling this way. Sometimes they take to alcohol, drugs, eating disorders, having flashbacks, nightmares, that type of thing.

135

British Victims of Abortion lists 30 possible symptoms of 'post-abortion syndrome' including the creation of a phantom child, sleep disturbances, phobias, broken relationships and infertility.

These dramatic claims are questioned by Mary Boyle, a psychologist at the University of East London. In the *Psychologist* journal she writes:

> Research on the effects of abortion is fraught with methodological problems, but there is no clear evidence that legal abortion, particularly in the early stages of pregnancy, carries significant physical or psychological risks. But whatever risks do exist cannot be assumed to be intrinsic to abortion and our evaluation of them must take account of the impact of social attitudes to abortion on the responses of individual women. And risks of negative reactions to abortion also have to be balanced against the physical and psychological risks from childbirth and the psychological risks of being refused an abortion.[2]

Research suggests that the women who are most likely to suffer the greatest psychological distress after an abortion have prior children, prior abortion(s), low self-esteem, late abortions, a maternal orientation, strong religious beliefs, lack of relationship support, have been coerced into an abortion, or have prior emotional problems.

I found little evidence of 'post-abortion syndrome' among the fifteen interviewees who had had terminations. They seemed as comfortable as one can be about making a decision that is so ethically and morally loaded, and felt that it was the right choice for them.

I had two abortions before my husband. One pregnancy was the result of a rape. The abortions were unpleasant, like going to a dentist, but bang, it was done and finished. (Marie, 44)

I had an abortion two years ago. I was upset obviously, but made the decision the minute I knew I was pregnant. The doctor offered me counselling, but I didn't really need it: I had already made my decision. My breasts started to feel really swollen and hard when I was pregnant. After I took the test I kept thinking: my God, there's a baby inside me; in another few months my whole body will be changing shape. I felt scared: I'm not in control of my body. I didn't feel I was going to get attached to what was inside me in any way. Relief was my main feeling after the abortion. (Angie, 27)

Afterwards I had none of the angst or depression that one reads about, just tremendous relief. I didn't think I'd killed a child, it wasn't emotional in that sense. (Josephine, 63)

I got pregnant when I changed my pill and I was horrified. My immediate thought was that I don't want this to be happening to me, and I was angry about the situation. I didn't feel any guilt at all: it was a bundle of cells or my ruined life. I don't put a great deal of value on what I did: it wasn't anything major, I don't feel I destroyed a life. I was just three months pregnant; if it had been later I think it would have been emotionally harder to make the decision. Being pregnant made me think a bit more deeply about not wanting children, and really confirmed in me that I didn't want them. (Dianne, 28)

The feeling of their body being invaded or taken over was common among those who'd had abortions. The foetus was an unwelcomed intrusion, 'having something inside that isn't you, living and feeding off you. That's a strange idea I'm not prepared to take on,' says one woman. 'I felt that my body had been invaded by a parasite; this thing growing inside me and I couldn't do anything. I couldn't wait to get rid of it,' says another.

They also expressed considerable anxiety about their bodies changing shape and being 'out of control'. For many, like Dianne, the experience of early pregnancy crystallised thoughts about not wanting children: it was a time when they explored their feelings at a deeper level. Janette, a 30-year-old legal secretary, has been married for twelve years. When they first married, she and her husband didn't discuss having a family. 'I suppose there was an assumption we would have children, but we were really young and just happy to be with each other.' Over the years their opinions have fluctuated, and the subject has been a source of conflict. Janette's husband feels much more strongly than she that he doesn't want to be a parent. 'I suppose I am deferring to his way of thinking because the relationship is very important; however, I do agree with him,' says Janette. The statement is a confused one, and what is probably more revealing is the way Janette felt two years ago when she accidentally became pregnant. 'It was a big decision to make and we talked about it a lot. It was funny, I was the one who was most adamant that we shouldn't have it. He was the one saying I don't know what we should do, and I was the one who made firm decision. When it came down to it, when I was pregnant, I realised that I didn't want to have a child.

There were all these different things I wanted to do, and I wouldn't be able to do them all with a child: I felt as if part of my life had ended.'

Abortion seems to be less traumatic for women who have already thought about whether or not they want children, and are clear that motherhood isn't for them. Yet even the woman who has thoroughly rationalised her decision might suddenly find herself experiencing dramatic mixed feelings. Marion, a 41-year-old journalist, who has had two abortions, found that the experience became more difficult with age. 'I first got pregnant when I was 22. I'd just left home and he was a chap I was working with. Initially when I got pregnant I was quite pleased that I could do it, but I didn't want the child. I wasn't grown up enough. He was married, and there was never any question of me having it. I found it a bit traumatic, emotionally it was difficult, but you're very resilient when you're young; your instincts are quite strong, and mine told me it was the right thing to do.'

Marion got pregnant again in her late twenties, but again the circumstances weren't right: 'It was another married man, who would actually have been quite happy for me to have the child. I was living at home at the time to save money and didn't want to have it. It didn't seem right to bring a child into the world under those circumstances. I've got rigid ideas about what a child should have, and I don't really think that being a single parent is a good idea.' After the abortion Marion had what she calls a 'horrible time with hormones'. Her dramatic reaction to the abortion took her by surprise: 'It would affect me when I saw a small child; it would hit home. It was very alien for me to have these feelings, it was obviously my hormones working, maternal feelings were coming out. I

139

was at an airport in Spain and had been on holiday to recuperate and I saw this baby, and ridiculously thought I'd snatch it. It was a temporary moment of madness. The feelings didn't linger, they went. I brushed them aside.'

Almost all of the women I interviewed said they would have an abortion if they discovered they were pregnant. 'I'd go straight to the doctor and have an abortion. No way would I contemplate going through with it,' says one. A few, however, felt that such an action would be ethically wrong. '1 went on the pill and was very careful until my husband's vasectomy was confirmed successful. If I had been pregnant it would have been a difficult decision, not because at the back of my mind I'd really want a child, but because I'd have to live with having "killed" a possible innocent life,' says 32-year-old Sally. Miriam, 33, has similar feelings: 'I wouldn't have an abortion because I don't agree with it. Murdering a kid would always be on my mind and I'd have to put it up for adoption.'

Many expressed a real fear of pregnancy, and are thrown into terrible anxiety if their periods are late. 'I was forever buying pregnancy testing kits, even if I was just one day late,' says one. Despite the reliability of modern contraception, false alarms were reported as common. 'They scare the life out of me,' says 26-year-old Elizabeth, a theatrical agent who lives with her partner, an actor. 'My periods are quite irregular anyway if I'm stressed or there's a change of routine. I tend to panic more than necessary. The most overdue I've been is two weeks. I'd go straight to the doctor and have an abortion: no way would I contemplate going through with it.' Maria, a 29-year-old journalist, is in a steady relationship with a personnel manager, and recently had a pregnancy scare: 'I thought, "Oh my God": I would have to have an abortion, this is going to freak me out. Every time I have a period it's like a celebration to me. I run around and do a celebration dance.'

When she was seventeen, Emily, now 22, tested out her feelings about pregnancy by not using proper contraception: 'I ran away from home to live with my first boyfriend Martin, who was 23. I gave up my A levels and took this grotty job as a receptionist so that I could be with him. I was playing at being an adult, trying to be grown up. He used to say he wanted me to have six children and I was so flattered. Half of me wanted to be pregnant, we took lots of risks, I was gambling in a way. I wanted to have that proud feeling: look what I can do. When I did get my period there would be this sense of relief. I realise now it was a cop-out because I didn't know what I wanted out of life.'

Two of the women I spoke to feel that their fear of pregnancy contributes to their reticence with men. Katrin, a 27-year-old au pair from East Germany says, 'If I got pregnant I'd have an abortion, that would be my first thought. This is probably a reason why I like to stay away from men, not to have this problem in the first place.' Lucy, a 69-year-old retired civil servant, didn't have a relationship with a man until she was 30. 'Quite early in my life I decided I wasn't going to have anything to do with men,' she says. 'I think this was from reading stories in magazines where it seemed to me all the troubles arose from girls having relationships with men. It always seemed that a woman got into a situation which she found very difficult to retrieve herself from because of either having a marriage or a child.'

Sterilisation

Surprisingly, sterilisation is the most popular form of contraception in Britain (and the world), with female and male sterilisations combined knocking the pill from its number one slot as the favoured form of birth control. In 1970 a survey of family planning services in England and Wales found that only 4 per cent of married couples had been sterilised. This figure has leapt dramatically over the ensuing years: the General Household Survey of 1989 put the total of women aged 16–49 and their partners who have been sterilised for contraceptive reasons at 23 per cent (22 per cent take the pill). There are several reasons for this change in trend: sterilisation became a lot easier to obtain on the NHS (although this has now changed), and for women the operation became simpler with the introduction of the laparoscopic technique. This is a less intrusive procedure than general surgery and can be done under local anaesthetic.

There are currently two procedures for female sterilisation: the first, salpingectomy, requires a general anaesthetic. An incision is made in the lower abdomen, just above the pubic hairline, bringing the fallopian tubes into view. Part of each tube is cut out, and the ends tied, clamped or cauterised. The laparoscopic technique is often done under local anaesthetic. The abdomen is inflated with a harmless gas, which separates the internal organs so that the surgeon can see the fallopian tubes clearly. A small, lit, viewing instrument is inserted through the abdominal wall just below the navel, through which the fallopian tubes can be seen. Another small incision is made in the lower abdomen and the surgeon inserts electrical forceps to cauterise the tubes, or sealing

142

rings. In the near future, laser sterilisations may simplify the procedure even further.

A number of scares about the safety of the pill in the late 1970s and early 1980s forced women to look elsewhere for long-term contraception. 'I was sterilised a year ago. I was completely and utterly in no doubt. I had been on the pill for years and years and totally went off the idea of taking hormones, as I was getting older and had been an occasional smoker. Everything else isn't as safe, and I thought, what's the point? Why not finish it once and for all?' says one woman.

Male sterilisation, vasectomy, is simpler and quicker than female sterilisation. It is performed under local anaesthetic, sometimes by GPs. Two small incisions are made in the scrotum so that a small portion of each sperm-carrying duct can be cut out and tied. Thereafter, a man ejaculates in the normal way, although the semen will not contain sperm. This continues to be produced in the testicles where it eventually dissolves.

There is currently no comprehensive data on how many sterilisations are performed in Britain, but it is clear that despite their popularity, in recent years sterilisations have become increasingly hard to obtain on the NHS. Many health authorities have either stopped offering sterilisations, or severely cut back the service to save money, and couples are being forced to obtain the operation privately. Fees for a female sterilisation are around £400, and £150 for a vasectomy. The Family Planning Association sees this trend as 'very worrying', especially in some areas of the country where it is practically impossible to be sterilised without going privately. 'The NHS is actually obliged and supposed to be providing all these different methods of contraception, yet it's not providing sterilisation, particularly female sterilisation,' says Ruth Grigg of the Family Planning Association. Child-free women are probably the first to suffer from these cutbacks. 'A woman who didn't have any children might not be seen as a priority for sterilisation, whereas I suspect a mother of eight would find it a lot easier,' says Grigg. Eleven of the women I interviewed had been sterilised, and a further eight had partners who'd had vasectomies (there was also one couple who preferred not to reveal which one had been sterilised). Additionally there were four women who, with their partners, were actively seeking sterilisation. Many reported problems in having the operation on the NHS; some had gone privately, others have given up for the time being.

The '120' rule

Until recently it would probably have been impossible for a child-free woman to be sterilised. If a woman wanted it, her doctor would multiply her age by the number of children she had. If the result came to 120 or more her request would be granted. By this reckoning, a woman who didn't want children, or wanted very few, would be either post-menopausal or dead by the time she qualified according to the '120 rule'. Because of the finality of sterilisation the women and men having the operations are older. According to the Family Planning Association, in 1989 only 1 per cent of women aged 16–24 had been sterilised compared to 46 per cent of those aged 40–44. It is fairly rare for a woman who has no children to be sterilised: only 3 per cent compared with 45 per cent of women who have three or more children. Many younger women who approached their doctors for sterilisation were told to wait until they were 30. Although there are no national guidelines, this was generally deemed to be the age when a woman can seriously make such a decision about her reproductive life. A recent article in *Doctor* magazine also puts the divisive age at 30, saying that sterilisation is not recommended for younger women, women with no children, or those who are single. On the whole, doctors are understandably cautious about sterilisation referrals: a 1985 survey of counselling services for sterilisation found that young women – with or without children – were likely to be dissuaded by their doctors. However, many of the women who were turned down by their doctors continued to pursue the operation and 40 per cent were successful.

'The first doctor we approached, a woman, said I was too young at 26. She suggested that if my husband were to die I might remarry and want children with that partner,' says Patricia, a 34-year-old secretary. 'Nothing I said would persuade her otherwise. The second doctor we approached, male, didn't bat an eyelid. He said he respected me for knowing my own mind, and made an appointment for us both at the local family planning clinic. The staff at the family planning clinic were obviously worried that we were so young, and went into a huddle several times to discuss us, but we stuck to our guns, and our decision was accepted.'

Emily, a 37-year-old married office temp, was similarly persistent in her request: 'It took many years to convince doctors that I was serious about not having children. I was 30 when I found a doctor willing to sterilise me. He was very good and very kind, but I really had to convince him that I would not change my mind, before he would agree to the operation.'

'I asked the Family Planning Association about sterilisation when I was 19 – they said wait until you're 30,' says Sarah, now 33 and married. 'I had it done for my 31st birthday by asking them to "throw it in" with a cervical biopsy.'

The counselling procedure

Although operations to reverse the procedure are possible, sterilisation has to be viewed as permanent, and as such needs a great deal of thought. Dr Gerald Worcester, a consultant psychotherapist at St George's Hospital, London, has treated women who regret their decision. In an interview in *Doctor*,[3] he says that counselling beforehand is essential because 'many women do not fully realise the reasons behind their seeking sterilisation. They may be trying to punish themselves or they may want the decision of whether to have children taken away from them because they are frightened of the responsibility.'

Liz Davies, manager of a Marie Stopes clinic, a charitable organisation that offers contraceptive advice, abortions and sterilisations, has counselled many women and men. She is child-free and as she was sterilised at 30, feels that she has a particular empathy with women who don't want children. Many child-free women approach clinics like the Marie Stopes when they have been unable to obtain a sterilisation on the NHS. 'We would never refuse anyone sterilisation, regardless of age, marital status, whether she's got children or not,' says Davies. 'That's our policy: however, women under 25 we feel should be given a bit more space to make the decision. We would only refuse someone if we felt they were unsure, and it was totally the wrong thing for them.' A Marie

Stopes clinic usually offers a sterilisation 'consultation', and if all goes well, the operation can be performed on the same day. With younger women, and those who are child-free, Davies prefers to arrange a successive consultation with a time gap of anything between two weeks to three months. She points out that women and men who approach the clinic have already read the brochure, have usually thought through their decision, and are not in consultation to try and make up their minds, but to initiate proceedings.

Clients are seen individually, or in couples, whichever they prefer. It used to be necessary for married partners to sign a consent form before sterilisation, but in July 1991 the British Medical Association agreed that an individual should be able to make his or her own decision. During the 45-minute consultation Davies talks about the woman's reason for sterilisation, what's brought about the decision, the kind of contraception she is currently using, what her alternatives may be, and how her partner (if she has one) feels about it.

'We do see quite a number of women who don't have children and have never wanted them,' says Davies. 'If they're in a relationship I ask them to think about how they'd feel if their relationship broke up and they formed a new relationship with someone who wants children. I want to know why she feels she doesn't want children: sometimes it's a fear of pregnancy; sometimes a bad experience in the past. I really need to know she's making an objective decision. I ask her to think about the implications of suddenly getting very broody in ten years' time – it does happen.' For Davies, alarm bells sound if the woman dwells too much on the possibility of reversal, and if her decision has been sudden. "How long have you considered this?" is a key question,' she says. 'I'm also concerned if she wants sterilisation at the same time as a termination. She may not be making an objective decision, and asking to be sterilised in reaction to an unwanted pregnancy.'

The youngest child-free woman Liz Davies has referred for sterilisation was 19 years old. 'When she first came she was 18 and we counselled her at length three times because we weren't happy. We kept telling her to think about it some more and come back in three months, and each time she came back to us at exactly the right time saying, "I still want it done". She was absolutely sure and very mature. At the age of 19 we did it, and we haven't heard from her since saying she'd regretted the decision. She'll be in her mid twenties now.'

Some people would argue that 19 is far too young to make such a major decision. Few women feel ready to have a baby while they are still in their teens, but their emotions have developed and changed enormously by their mid-twenties. Liz Davies argues that you can't prejudge a woman, and you have to respect that she knows her own mind. At the age of 18 Davies knew that she never wanted children, and believes that now, at 40, she is unlikely to change. 'I have never regretted being sterilised,' she says. Controversially she argues that 'a woman has the right to make that decision, even if it subsequently turns out to be the wrong decision. I don't think we've got the right to refuse, as long as we're sure she knows all the implications.'

Sally, 32, a customer services adviser for a building society, is married and her husband had a vasectomy seven years ago. She describes the counselling proce-dure: 'My husband went to the doctor, who was very

understanding, and then we went to a counsellor which we paid for. She was a woman, and asked whether we wanted to see her individually, which we didn't. I suppose they have to make sure nobody is being pressurised. We were with her for half an hour, and she asked me how I'd feel if I discovered I was pregnant. She seemed quite satisfied we were making the right decision. When I told a friend of mine she said it might be the worst decision we'd ever made. But surely to have a child and change your mind is worse? We've never regretted it, and our sex life is very good.'

Too final?

The majority of people (whether parents or not) don't regret being sterilised, but some do. As the numbers of women and men wanting sterilisation have increased, so has the number wanting reversals. It has been estimated that between 1 and 3 per cent of those undergoing a vasectomy request a reversal,[4] citing remarriage, death of children, change of heart and altered financial circumstances among their reasons. A study published in the *British Medical Journal* [5] found that over half of those men who requested a reversal were divorced or separated and felt that their future relationships were impeded by their infertility. Most requests came from the under-35s, who'd had the operation at a time of emotional crisis.

According to another *British Medical Journal* study,[6] women are more likely to regret the decision than men. Figures suggest that about 10 per cent express some regret, although less than 5 per cent actually go as far as asking for a reversal. Those who are most likely to want a

reversal were under 30 when sterilised, have an unstable marriage and, interestingly, tend to be working class.

Although counsellors like Liz Davies stress that sterilisation must be thought of as irrevocable, the chances of a reversal are quite good and about 50–70 per cent of women go on to achieve pregnancy with a new partner: between 40–50 per cent of men are successful.

Despite this success rate, when making the decision whether or not to have children, sterilisation represents the end of discussion: the lid is shut on the issue. Some see sterilisation as an unhealthy denial of possibility. 'Voluntary sterilisation implies that no fundamental changes will be allowed to take place – life's die has been cast. It is the abandonment of management of one's own fertility and a regression to child status. Sterilisation is not a substitute for contraception because it is the destruction of fertility: it makes as much sense as blinding a man who needs glasses,' writes Germaine Greer in *Sex and Destiny*.[7] One could argue that Greer's objections hold little practical value for the mother of five children who no longer wants to be a slave to her fertility. Greer herself has no children, and her anxiety about sterilisation seems more appropriate for the child-free woman who is denying for ever the growth of her own desire to experience motherhood. Many child-free women would agree with Greer that sterilisation is simply too final. 'There's a big part of me that wants children, so sterilisation is out of the question,' says Emily, 22.

Of those women who are not sterilised (or their partners) very few said they were 100 per cent sure they didn't want children. Even those who are adamant rate their certainty at 99 per cent, with the remaining 1 per

cent allocated to 'Well, you never know, I *might* change my mind,' or 'Maybe one day I'll wake up desperately broody.' Sue, a 33-year-old single journalist, adds that blocking that route so unequivocally might lead to a dramatic U-turn: 'No, I wouldn't be sterilised. Everything is ambiguous and ambivalent, and not to admit that you might change is dangerous, too rigid. I therefore feel more confident that my attitudes are somehow enduring because I'm not completely closed off to all other ideas, otherwise it would be very extreme, and as we know, extremes change into their opposite.'

> I've never thought of sterilisation. A friend mentioned it to me the other night, and it had never occurred to me before. I think it's too final. (Coral, 43)

> All I can say is that I don't want to become a mother at the moment, but I know that there is a side of me that is very maternal and wants children. Sterilisation would deny that part of myself for ever. (Penny, 30)

> I've thought about sterilisation, but at the moment I don't need to. That's something so final. (Marnie, 31)

> I haven't really thought about it. I've been very lucky with the coil. The first one was in for eleven years. If I'd had lots of problems I would probably have thought about it, but it's a very dramatic thing to do. (Marion, 41)

> We have thought about sterilisation but would rather leave things as they are. Neither of us wants to be 'tampered with'. We find present arrangements quite satisfactory. (Julia, 32)

A difference of opinion

Because it denies the possibility of change, sterilisation also might cause difficulties in a relationship where one partner feels more ambivalent about not having children than the other. For Janet, 29, a mature student, her husband of five years is not as equally committed to being child-free. Sterilisation would force them to face a perplexing matter of contention that could end their relationship: 'I would have no objections to being sterilised, but my husband is totally against the idea. The finality of it horrifies him; although he knows he will probably never be a father, he likes to know that the physical possibility is there: he wants to keep our options open, even if we never exercise them. In principle I can understand that: I've never been one to shut off options unnecessarily. On the other hand, shutting this particular door, knowing that finally the issue was resolved beyond any possible doubt, would be a tremendous relief to me. It's a thorny issue, that I feel can only complicate our position further at this stage, and I'm happy to leave it in the background for the time being.'

It works both ways Janette, a 30-year-old legal secretary, has gone through phases of wanting children, but her husband is steadfast in his commitment to the child-free lifestyle. Sometimes Janette feels she is deferring to her husband because the relationship is more important. At other times she believes that the decision is truly shared. Sterilisation is not suited to such ambivalence. 'He would have a vasectomy if it was his decision,' explains Janette, 'but he's thinking of me, just in case we change our minds.'

152

Finality means freedom

For some women the finality of sterilisation comes as a great relief. No longer do they have to juggle with the issues or worry about possible pregnancies. 'As I was being wheeled to the theatre a very nice doctor kept saying, "Are you sure? You can still change your mind",' says 29-year-old Jane who was sterilised a year ago. Jane, a systems programmer, says she's always known that she wouldn't have children, and that she and her husband 'enjoy life as a couple and don't need a third person around'. Although she was on the pill, Jane lived with a constant fear of pregnancy. 'I used to buy pregnancy tests all the time. I was horrified if my period was late and would imagine my world falling apart. I had been on the pill for years and went off the idea of taking hormones, especially as I was getting older. Everything else isn't as safe, and I thought, what's the point? Why not finish it once and for all.' Since the operation Jane is no longer anxious about an unwanted pregnancy. 'I've never looked back,' she says. 'I'm free, completely free.'

Terri's husband had already had a vasectomy when she met him. She believes that their shared views are partly the reason they were attracted to each other. Terri, 33, gets very annoyed when their choice to remain child-free is not taken seriously. 'People always say, "You'll change your mind",' says Terri. The fact that her husband has had a vasectomy is like the final trump card. 'In that situation I'll often tell them that my husband has had a vasectomy. That soon shuts them up!' For Terri the finality of sterilisation alleviates the social pressures placed upon her and her husband to start a family. Jane expresses a similar sentiment: 'My sterilisation shut a few friends up who said maybe I would change my mind. I got a bit more respect, which is really good.'

Liz Davies similarly finds that the finality of sterilisation frees her from pressures: 'I was divorced and wasn't looking for another relationship,' she says, 'but it was always in the back of my mind that if I did meet somebody, what happens if he really wants children and I don't? If I'm sterilised then there's no argument: he has to accept it, or not. I'm not going to be pressurised. A lot of women want to be sterilised as an insurance policy that they're not going to be pressurised into having a child they don't want.'

Her or him

How do couples decide who should be sterilised? The ratio of female to male sterilisations has been changing since 1970. Despite the fact that vasectomy is a simpler operation than female sterilisation, traditionally the woman usually has the operation. In 1970 seven women had been sterilised for every three men who had vasectomies. By 1976 that ratio had narrowed to seven women to every six men, and today the figures are roughly equal. The department of obstetrics and gynaecology at the University of Aberdeen analysed the various reasons for couples choosing vasectomy instead of female sterilisation: some had done so because the woman risked health complications (such as high blood pressure); men had felt that their partner had done her share in terms of contraception, and now it was their turn; some wives were unwilling to be sterilised either through fear or because they believed it was their husband's turn to take contraceptive responsibility; for nearly half the couples both were willing to be sterilised but the hospital waiting lists for vasectomies were shorter. The reasons for female sterilisation included wives who felt that no matter what the future held they didn't want more children while the husbands might; nearly half the husbands were unwilling to consider vasectomy because of fear of 'losing their manhood'; and in a few cases the waiting lists were shorter. According to a study in the *Journal of Biosocial Science*, 'choice ultimately depends on the relative attitudes of men and women to responsibility for contraception, to ideas about sexuality and fertility and the experience of men and women known to them who have been sterilised'.[8]

When an agreement is reached, inequality in how strongly each partner feels can determine who has the operation. Miriam, 33, says she first contemplated never having children when she was still at school, and made a firm decision at 19. She cites loss of privacy and freedom as her major reasons. She admits to a violent temper which she fears would not make her a good mother. 'I have a violent streak and a vicious temper when wound up. I would start to beat the child as I was beaten when I was a child,' she says. Miriam has been married for thirteen years, and believes that her strong feelings against parenthood have influenced her husband. 'He never really questioned the assumption that he would have kids until he met me. I convinced him with no trouble,' she says. 'I was on the pill and didn't think anything else was sufficiently reliable. I knew I wouldn't have an abortion if I got pregnant as I don't believe in it. I was all right on the pill, then after a couple of years I started getting thrush continually, for three or four years, then he started getting it too. I said, "This is hopeless, there's nothing else for it."

155

He was terrified of operations, but I've had a couple and knew I could handle it. Also I knew I would not have children, whereas I thought if I get run over by a bus, you might change your mind if you're with some woman and she desperately wants a family. I won't relent so I'm the one who ought to have it done.' Miriam was sterilised at 25, and had to go privately because she couldn't persuade an NHS doctor to refer her at such a young age.

Amelia, 22, is adamant about her decision as she feels children would jeopardise her career in the civil service. 'I know I couldn't do both and would resent the child for having to give it up.' She has been living with her partner for four years; he is 'not completely opposed to having children', but doesn't want them enough to end the relationship. 'He's probably not unhappy not to have them.' She has already discussed the possibility of sterilisation with her doctor because she doesn't feel that the pill is safe enough. After some thought she believes that she should be the one to have the operation, not her partner. 'I asked him about a vasectomy quite early on after we had been living together for a year, but he's pathologically terrified of it. I wondered if this was something to do with him wanting to have children, really. Thinking about it, I know that I definitely don't want to have children. I feel it's unlikely that we should ever split up, but if we did, he could meet someone who really wants children, and therefore it would be unfair of me to insist he has a vasectomy.'

Who knows?

Some couples prefer to keep this very personal decision private. Many were prepared to tell friends, but felt more cautious about family and 'would-be' grandparents. 'All my friends know, but nobody in the family knows: it's too heinous a crime,' says Jane, 29, a married systems programmer who was sterilised a year ago. 'I think it's probably kinder to let my mother live in hope. I feel it would cause her worry: have you done the right thing, what if you change your mind? She's had three major back operations and is in a lot of pain, so I don't want to upset her further.'

Sally, 32, also feels that her mother would be upset if she knew that her husband had had a vasectomy. 'There has never been a situation when it was right to tell her. I've made it quite clear that we won't have children, but she still thinks we will have them. She's 70 and assumes that once you're married it's the natural course: she never had the choice. I think she's doubtful about vasectomy anyway because my brother had two children and then had a vasectomy. His marriage went wrong and he married again and had it reversed. My mother thought this was a wonderful thing.'

Other women decided that they would like to share the fact that they or their partners have been sterilised, although the news may not be welcomed. 'I did wonder, but in the end told my mum that Alex was going to have a vasectomy,' says 23-year-old Katy, an administrator at a nuclear power plant. 'She just sort of looked at me with her mouth open. She didn't think we were serious about not having children up until that point. Then she said, "Well, it's your life, and you can't have children to please me and your dad". She told my dad and he was disappointed and upset. I've turned out so different to what they expected: I didn't live by the plan they had of me as a little girl.'

One couple had been sterilised but were unprepared to disclose who had had the operation. 'Nobody else knows, and do you mind if I don't tell you which one of us has been sterilised?' asks 36-year-old Karen, a musician. 'It's a very personal decision; we're romantic and feel it's something very private to the two of us. You don't go around telling people all about your sex life and what turns each other on. It's not because I'm afraid of people's reaction, but there are aspects of my life that are very special to myself and my partner and I'd like to keep them that way. There tends to be an element of ridicule when people are "snipped" or "chopped out" – I don't want to debase it in that way. It's something that was a very sincere decision.'

Terri, an extrovert woman who works as a staff training manager, takes a very different attitude to Karen about her husband's vasectomy, and enjoys dropping it into the conversation whenever possible. 'I'm always bringing it up in conversations in the pub or whatever. I like to see the look of surprise on their faces,' she says. Terri says she delights in being slightly unconventional and that she always knew she didn't want a traditional marriage.

Hysterectomy

According to the Office of Population Censuses and Surveys 66,000 women have hysterectomies each year in Britain. Statisticians have estimated that by the age of 75 one in five women have had a hysterectomy: it is one of the most common major operations a woman can have. The surgical removal of any part of our body can involve feelings of loss and grief but for many women hysterectomy has an especially emotional significance. Studies have reported psychiatric disturbances in up to 70 per cent of patients following a hysterectomy, although most women recover within one to three years. One woman interviewed in a magazine feature about hysterectomy expressed her feelings very vividly when she said, 'I felt absolutely hollow. I felt like a grapefruit which had been cut open and had all the juice, all the flesh, all the goodness scooped out.' This particular woman was a 42-year-old mother, but what sort of reaction do child-free women have to hysterectomy? 'Because I had spent my entire fertile life trying to control my uterus with hormones and coils, it came as quite a shock to me when I got so upset about my hysterectomy. I thought to myself that I should be grateful that I would never have an unwanted pregnancy. It's true, that has been a relief, but I also felt that something very womanly about me had been taken away,' said one 45-year-old.

Dianne, a 28-year-old press officer, feels little emotional attachment to her uterus. She suffers from menorrhagia (painful heavy periods) and, having tried several treatments with no success, is now seeking a hysterectomy. Each year 20,000 women have their wombs removed because of menorrhagia. To those who would feel bereft at the loss of their reproductive organs this seems a drastic solution, but Dianne, who says she has never wanted children, seems to feel no special attachment: 'When I asked my doctor the reaction was total horror. She said I wouldn't be able to have a hysterectomy until I was 35, because she sees so many women who decide to be sterilised who then go back and try to have it reversed. There is no way that they would do it until I'm nearly past the stage of being able to have children should I want to. I'm angry: it's my body and

I know I don't want children. I could go and get an abortion if I wanted one, and yet I can't take a step that would stop me getting pregnant permanently. I've asked my doctor four times in the past six months, but she thinks it's a radical, almost unthinkable solution. I'll keep trying and maybe go private if that's an option.'

Maud, 75, met similar resistance. 'When I went through my menopause I had a terrible, shocking time. It went on and on and I was terribly ill. I used to lose so much blood I had to have a blood transfusion. I kept asking my gynaecologist for a hysterectomy, but she said I still might want children. In the end I went in for a D and C, and she said if the bleeding doesn't stop in two months I'll give you a hysterectomy straight away. The bleeding stopped, and then I had peace of mind because I knew I was never going to have a baby.'

6

CHILD-FREE WOMEN AND
THEIR RELATIONSHIPS

M OST women marry: it is an expected part of their
biography, and the vast majority tie the knot at least
once. The popularity of marriage is declining dramatically
however: in 1971 only 4 per cent of women remained
unmarried by the age of 50, but by 1987 the proportion
had grown to 17 per cent. Women today are older when
they marry, marry less, and often have fewer children, if
any at all. The institution is also less stable: nearly one in
two marriages formed today will be on the rocks within
the next fifteen years; one in five children have divorced
parents by the age of 16, and one in four are born out
of wedlock. Such changes have long stirred moral panic:
any loosening of the family structure raises immediate
concern about social disintegration and falling moral standards. 'Marriage is out of fashion,' shouts the front cover
of the *Daily Express*, in response to a 1993 report from the
Family Policy Studies Centre, showing that the number of

161

weddings has dropped to its lowest level since the Second World War. Alarmists point to the royal family, hit by divorce and separation, suggesting that the rot has infiltrated even the most privileged and traditional echelons of society.

Women who choose not to marry, or who choose to remain child-free, are also seen as perpetrators of family breakdown and declining standards. But what is viewed as one person's moral decline can be seen as another's liberation: are social structures slipping downhill, or are they simply changing? Are they breaking up, rather than breaking down?

'The growth of divorce may not connote the trivialisation of marriage but its increased significance, with more intolerance of imperfections and the unremitting search for the right partner,' suggests sociologist Joan Chandler in *Women without Husbands*.[1] Increased access to divorce and the growth of the nuclear family means that modern marriage is based less on extended family networking and more on personal fulfilment. Marriage has become a very insular, two-person affair. 'For us it's a very private matter, hence we only had two people at our wedding and nobody else even knew,' says Karen, a 36-year-old musician. She goes on to describe her very modern marriage with its roots in equality. 'Thereafter we function very much on the philosophy of teamwork. Whoever is around at the time gets and does the requisite chores. We are both busy, professional people and I can't be doing with the business of my husband expecting his shirts ironed and meals cooked. Fortunately, neither can he. Just as well, when I'm away for weeks on end in Japan, the USA, etc.'

Increasingly a woman has a choice: if a relationship is

unhappy she may have the economic power which makes it easier for her to leave it and she may also have the social support to enable her to do so. Gone are the days when a divorced woman hung her head in disgrace. Joan Chandler points out that growing numbers of women inhabit what she calls the 'margins of marriage'. These are women who cohabit, those who do not regularly live with their husbands, single women who have been married and who are now either widowed or divorced, and women who choose to avoid marriage. Child-free women inhabit all of these 'margins', and they can also be found in regular marital relationships. It is among this latter group, the married child-free women, that there are extremely high expectations of personal satisfaction within their relationships. When asked what they looked forward to, first on the list for many was 'to continue being happy with my husband'.

Finding a like-minded partner

In a society where the expectation is largely that a romantic relationship will ultimately lead to marriage and children, relationships can be a fraught affair. 'When I meet guys in the pub and tell them I don't want children they look at me like I was some sort of vampire or something,' complains one woman. 'Men can't believe that a woman doesn't want children. They assume I must be really hard or something,' says another. Traditionally, men have prized women because of their potential to make them fathers, produce heirs, sons to work the land and daughters to tend them in their old age. Many women felt that their decision to remain child-free seriously jeopardised their chances of dating, and had found that relationships were frequently cut short when the subject of

children arose. Marie, 44, a divorcee, is currently breaking up with her partner of five years because he wants a
child. 'He's 49, and I think we are too old anyway. He's
changed his views and didn't want them when we started
seeing each other. Good luck to him. I hope he will find
somebody, but not me.' Marnie's eight-year relationship
eventually broke up because of similar disagreements. 'I
got to the point where I knew it couldn't go on as he was
wasting more and more time,' she says. 'We didn't really
discuss it. I would just say, "No, I don't want one" and
he'd say, "Go on, I'll look after it." He would have, too.
He was really nice, the boy-next-door type, dependable,
loyal, all the rest of it. The thought of having a child with
him scared me because I thought I'd have to be the really
traditional housewife type.'

Relationship counsellors encourage couples who are in
conflict to share their feelings, negotiate and find a
compromise. But the baby issue is beyond give-and-take:
it's impossible to have half a child. Relate (formerly
Marriage Guidance) says its counsellors regularly see
couples who are in dispute about parenthood, although
that isn't one of the most common reasons why couples
seek their help. 'We would look to see whether the couple
has discussed it and what they said at the time of marriage
or deciding to live together,' says Zelda West-Meads. All
too often, couples don't properly discuss the issue before
making a commitment to a relationship. 'There are many
couples who make assumptions of how it's going to be.
It's absolutely vital that whether you're going to have
children should always be discussed,' says West-Meads.
Counselling explores the views of each partner. 'If a
woman doesn't want children there would be no pressure
on her to change her mind, but an opportunity to see

whether there are any reasons she's aware of. Is it that she was the eldest child and the arrival of a new baby led to unconscious feelings of displacement? Or had she felt she wasn't very loved as a child, or a mistake? She may say that a baby takes up too much time, but there may be deeper reasons.' West-Mead's line of enquiry suggests an emphasis on unresolved past experiences, although she adds that the woman 'may look at these reasons and still not want children'. Relate admits that in some cases the only way forward is to help the couple recognise that the relationship cannot survive. 'One partner's need for children is so strong that either she's going to have to capitulate or he's going to resent it. In the end that destroys relationships.'

It destroyed Bethany's four-year marriage. When she married at 22, Bethany felt ambivalent about whether she wanted children, but knew for sure that she wouldn't plan to have them within the next seven or eight years. 'I had just started teaching and was very career minded and had my eye on a head of department position. I thought I might change my attitude, and people kept saying that when I'd been married a few years I'd change my mind.' She thought that she and her fiancé had discussed the issue and that he felt the same. 'Unfortunately as soon as the ring was on my finger it was a different matter,' says Bethany. 'He started to flush my pills down the toilet, saying, "Enough of all that, isn't it time you settled down and had a family?"' Bethany claims he was intensely jealous of her career and very possessive. 'He really wanted me barefoot and pregnant at the kitchen sink.' She attributes a lot of his views to their working-class East End background. 'That was the high expectation within the community, that within a year of getting married you would have a family. I don't know whether he came under a lot of pressure from his mother.' Ironically the same background fed Bethany's reluctance: 'The drudgery: I'd grown up with all these negative images of really young girls pushing prams with lots of kids and no money or hope of getting out of the situation.' She had been the first in her family to go on to higher education and wanted a career in order to avoid that trap. Eventually her husband's raids on her contraceptive pills became so bad that Bethany hid them at school. They argued constantly and then he became violent. At this point she left the marriage. 'It was such a relief to be out of the situation.'

Marion, 41, has never married, preferring to have many relationships, and seems pragmatic about her current partnership with a younger man of 22 which she believes will eventually end because of the issue of children. 'He would have a child. He said to me before: "Why don't you have your coil taken out?" I don't want a kid. There isn't a future for us because he wants children. He likes to think that he'll be in my life no matter what, which is a very nice thought. I've often tried to break it off because I can't see the point of it any more but he always comes back. I suppose it's one of those relationships that will carry on until it's finished. It hasn't been easy.'

Living with difference

Sometimes couples manage to live with their differences, but often they pay an extremely high price. What anguish there must be behind one woman's story that her husband secretly rubbed sperm into the inside of her pyjamas in the hope that she might become pregnant. The breakdown in communication, signalled by this quietly desperate act, is quite typical of the couples who disagree about starting a family. Laura, 43, describes how she and her husband gradually stopped talking about the issue: 'My husband loves children and kept talking about starting a family early in our marriage, even though he knows my thoughts. When we talked about getting married I told him I didn't want children. He doesn't talk about having children any more and has not done so for some years, but he still likes them. I can tell in the way he looks at them when we are outside.'

Such relationships survive on a knife edge: a precarious balance of desires and needs that couples try to deny or put on hold lest they topple the relationship. Janette's husband feels more strongly about not being a parent. 'It does cause conflict for me. I know how strongly he feels and I do agree with him, most of what he says. It's difficult for us to talk about it because it always ends up unresolved, really,' she says sadly. Part of Janette would like to be a mother, but she doesn't desire it strongly enough to bring about the end of her marriage; it's a loss she is trying to live with. Coral, 43, has been having a long-distance relationship with her African partner for thirteen years and talks of the unspoken unease between them on the subject: 'He would definitely like children and has made references to having children to leave money to and pass his name on. I think it is quite important to him culturally to have a baby. He's considered an oddity in that he's never married. I've made comments like, "It won't be me who has them." I don't know whether he has children back home in Africa, and frankly I don't want to know. If he does, as long as it doesn't impinge on his relationship with me I don't mind. In a way I'd be quite happy because I know he'd like that.

I suspect he hasn't: whether this is through not trying or bad luck is another matter entirely. I don't see any point in discussing it because that would be forcing an issue I don't particularly want to force. I think it might bust up our relationship if it were put openly.'

Janet, 29 and married five years, feels much more strongly than her husband about not having children, and describes the delicate balance of the situation: 'He grew up assuming he'd be a father, and is fond of children. He will sometimes talk about not thinking it right to leave no one behind when he dies, not to carry on the family name. I find these vague and unsatisfactory reasons for having children. He also talks about not having a family around him in old age, which does bother me, but not as much as it does him. He has deferred to me over this because he considers the relationship to be more important, but I know he still hopes I'll change my mind one day. I've often wondered what I'd do if he ever gave me an ultimatum, whether I'd really let him leave rather than have a child I didn't want. I'd wonder whether I was making a mountain out of a molehill, whether a family would really be so awful, and whether I was throwing away our relationship because of feelings that were completely misguided. On the other hand, I don't think the knowledge that he'd only stayed with me because I'd given him the child he wanted would do much for the relationship either. I feel that having a child under such circumstances would essentially destroy everything I value about us being together, that I'd lose him this way as much as if I'd let him walk away. I hope I'll never have to make this decision, that our present life without children will continue to be happy and fulfilling for my husband and he won't feel he needs babies to make it complete.'

Helen, 26, has been married for a year, and at the moment she and her husband are discussing their differences. 'My principle is held much more strongly, and we both believe that I should have the final word as it's my body.' Her husband Rob says that he is willing to go along with their child-free marriage, but when he gets drunk his desire to become a father surfaces, and Helen fears that this is how he feels at the deepest level. 'When he's drunk he gets sentimental and says he wants me to have his babies. There is a genuine wish there. There's a streak in him that is working-class macho and always will be. Time passes and the situation might change. There may be a situation one day where one wants a child and one doesn't. I am worried because you can never be completely sure about what the other one is thinking.'

Some women worry that a separation is simply being postponed, and that when they reach that now-or-never age the differences will prove uncontainable. A woman who has deferred to her partner may, at 35, suddenly feel a sense of panic as any hope she has of having a child fast diminishes. Likewise, a man who is deferring to his partner may feel that he is becoming too old to make a good father, and that his hopes and losses have to be faced head on. Amelia, 22, who lives with her boyfriend, feels certain she doesn't want to become a mother. Her boyfriend is rather more ambivalent. 'I made a definite point of bringing it up once we had decided to live together. He said when he was younger he always imagined that by 25 everyone was married and had two children. He said he didn't know if he was ready for the responsibility and didn't know whether he ever would be.' Amelia admits that she is worried that age will change his views: he is ten years older. 'I have been concerned that he does want children really and is either hoping I'll change my mind or putting up with it for the sake of our relationship. I'm concerned he might want them when he gets to 40 and I'm 30.

Georgina, 32, has experienced the same fears, although luckily her husband has become increasingly uninterested in parenthood during their eight-year marriage: I feel he defers to me because the relationship is so important to us both. But as he gets older and sees his nieces and nephews, he feels more and more that he would not want the trouble of kids.' Likewise, Rose, 42, has, with the passing years, become happier about being child-free. 'I'm deferring to my husband a little because he definitely does not want a child. He enjoys a good career in civil engineering and he loves me dearly; whereas I wouldn't have minded a child if one had come along earlier, but not now. I'm too involved in running and other hobbies and I like a peaceful home.'

Sharing the decision

Other couples are far more fortunate, saying that they share the decision not to have children. Sometimes these feelings were an initial point of attraction. Jill, now 36 and divorced, went on to meet the man she has been living with for the past ten years. As a consequence of the problem in her marriage, she says, parenthood was one of the first things they talked about. 'He'd been in a long-term relationship with a girl who wanted to settle him down and have babies,' says Jill. 'He was sure he didn't want babies. Meeting him was like hanging on to a life raft. It seemed so natural that we should be together.' Terri's husband had already had a vasectomy when they met. 'I'm sure it contributed to us getting together,' she said. Sally, 32, has been happily married for eleven years. Theirs was a whirlwind courtship: her husband proposed to her a few weeks after they met, and they moved in together within a month. 'We discussed everything under the sun in the first week, including children. It was a relief on both our parts to find out we feel the same. It possibly brought us together.

Here are the voices of four women describing how completely they share their child-free decision with their partner:

It is truly shared, however we have always said that should one of us wish to change our mind we would have a serious discussion about it. So far this has not been necessary and looks extremely unlikely. (Louise, 34, married eleven years)

We both share the same view over having children, we always have and always will. (Carolyn, 44, about to celebrate 24th wedding anniversary)

I don't want children and never have done. I have just asked my husband, once again, and he says, 'If you had a baby you'd be out of the door.' I think that answers the question! Neither of us can face the prospect. (Julia, 32, married eight years)

We have a really strong relationship and are happy together, so I can't see us splitting up. I was aware he didn't want children quite early on into the relationship. He was put into care as a child and then fostered, and he had to bring his three younger sisters up. He feels he's done his lot. (Elizabeth, 26, has been living with her boyfriend for six years)

These are not the only success stories. As the replies to my questionnaire began to come in, it became evident that there are many extremely happy child-free partnerships. The respondents, many of whom had been married for ten years or more, enthused unreservedly about their relationships: 'Getting married was the best decision I ever made. My marriage is very important to me and I don't really feel the need to add to it by having children,' says Debbie. 'Marriage is wonderful! It works because I've found the one-in-a-million person I'm truly compatible with,' says Linda.

Children can bring overwhelming joy to a relationship, but they can also cause terrible strain. There is a common belief that children stabilise a marriage and bond a couple, but in fact the birth of a first child is a notoriously difficult time, and marks a point when divorce rates soar. In *The Psychology of Happiness*[2] psychologist Michael Argyle charts the pattern of parental happiness: the graph takes a nose dive at the moment of the birth of a child, drops yet further when children are teenagers, and returns to normal when they have left home. Further psychological research published in France by Dr Gilbert Tordjman also suggests that marriage is at its happiest when a couple are in their fifties and sixties, and the children are no longer at home.[3] Statistics from the Office of Population Censuses and Surveys show that divorce rates are highest for marriages that have children under the age of 16, with 552 couples out of a thousand divorcing in 1990, whereas only 140 couples out of a thousand divorced when their children were over 16. Couples without children fall in between, with 307 divorces out of a thousand.

Many of the women said that they were extremely

happy and confirmed the view that a young child would disrupt their relationship. Being child-free gives couples a lot more time to themselves. Many pursue leisure activities together: weekends away, gardening, jogging, attending classic car rallies, golf, adult education, rambling, the list was long. The couples value the time they have to invest in each other, to enjoy making love without interruption, to have quiet romantic dinners and Sunday afternoons slouching together on the settee. 'We're just really happy with each other,' says Janette, 30, who has been happily married for twelve years. 'We're a bit scared that if we have children things will change and we wouldn't like it so much. There's no going back.'

Possessiveness can be the darker side of the 'two is company, three's a crowd' mentality. Would my partner love my child more than he or she loves me? 'My husband was an ambitious academic, and I think I married him because he was madly in love with me. When a man calls to a woman really very, very strongly and pursues her, she will give in. This is how it was for me. He said to me that if we were to have children he would be number two; he was very possessive,' says Marie, 44.

Debating the issue

Some couples thoroughly discussed the issue of children before becoming committed to their relationship. For many, however, assumption and luck played the bigger part. 'We didn't discuss it until we were nearly married, and only then very casually,' says Vicky, 37, who has been married for fifteen years. 'It was more luck that we agreed than active choice.'

Angie, 27, believes that she and her boyfriend of two and a half years have a mutual understanding, despite having never discussed their feelings about parenthood. 'Things are going really smoothly and its my best relationship so far,' she says. 'We haven't spoken about children at all. It's like one of these unspoken mutual decisions. I don't think he wants children. I've seen him with his sister's children and he doesn't play with them and has a short fuse.'

For someone like Sarah, 33, an unspoken agreement is far too risky and vague. She made a point of talking it over with her partner before agreeing to marry: 'We discussed it two years after we'd met. He told me he had no particular drive to be a father, at which point I knew I would be able to marry him fairly.'

The interviewees had mixed feelings about whether they could become involved deeply with someone who did want children. For those who feel ambivalent about becoming mothers, the right relationship could sway them. 'Theoretically, yes I could get involved with a man who wants children,' says Jo. 'A large part of a relationship is the sharing of ideas and it could be possible that someone could convince me to have a child if they felt strongly enough that it would enhance our relationship.' 'Maybe I'll want children if I meet the right man, someone who really believes in equal parenting. I've felt broody before with a previous boyfriend. Being in love does change you – maybe having a family will feel like the thing for us to do,' says Tanujah.

Marnie feels resolute, and from past experience has learnt that she couldn't become involved with a man who wants children, 'It's such a fundamental decision,' she says. 'You both really need to agree. My last boyfriend

174

loved me so much that he pretended he didn't want children and would have sacrificed the chance of father-hood to please me. It would never have worked out. I hated his subjugation.' Siobhan, 30 and single, agrees: 'It would be a problem. If I were to meet somebody new who I was very attracted to and it became apparent he had to have children I think it would put me off. That's the kind of pressure I don't want to live with. I could imagine being together with a man who already had children, that would be fine, although the role of stepmother is fraught with difficulties.'

Living on the margins of marriage

Being child-free gives a woman a lot more freedom to live on the margins of marriage, if that's the lifestyle she prefers. Without the responsibility of children she is considerably more independent, able to put her needs first, and to achieve economic self-sufficiency. The child-free woman is less pressurised into marriage. Maria, 29, has a long-term boyfriend with whom she's extremely happy, but doesn't want to marry. 'Marriage would change me. People fall into roles and at the moment I really like what I have and don't see any reason to change it. I can't think of a good enough reason to do it, what I'd gain from it. Marriage is an institution and generally women come off the worse for it,' she says. As a Greek Cypriot, she has come under considerable pressure from her family to marry. 'Nice Greek girls can't have relation-ships, you're meant to get married to them,' she explains. At one point the tensions were such that Maria broke off contact with her mother for several months. 'I kept saying: "Why is this a problem for you? It's not a problem for me." ' She has reached a precarious understanding with her family, who now accept the situation, but if she were to have children the pressures on her would be even greater. 'Having a baby out of marriage just isn't done.' Likewise Tanujah is pressurised by her Asian parents, who would like to arrange a marriage for her. 'Sometimes we're at a wedding and people come over with enquiries about me. My mum wants me to stand by her, but I walk off. At one point my mum said, "We've got to get you married." My community, the Jains, has a dating club for single professionals. My mum was insistent that I went, so I did once with my brother. It was a dinner and dance. I didn't like any of the men particularly; they were a bit staid for my liking. My mum said to me that over 25 I'm an old maid, not desirable goods any more.'

Amelia lives with her boyfriend and has no plans to marry. 'There are no moral or religious concerns, and since we're not going to have children we're not going to have to provide legal or moral stability. If I were to have children that's the only circumstance in which I feel I definitely would have to get married. It's easier for children if both parents have the same name and everything is legally tied up.'

Lucy, 69, spent most of her life in a relationship with a man who was separated but not divorced; had she wanted children, the situation would not have been tolerated by her generation. 'I didn't imagine myself being married; I suppose other girls did,' says Lucy. 'I remember walking with a schoolfriend and she said all she wanted was a husband, home and garden. She got what she wanted. This was her ambition when she was 12 years old. I was a bit vague about what I wanted, but I wanted a bit more than that. I wanted what I suppose you'd call a career.'

She had a career in the civil service for most of her working life, and was very shy of men, not having her first romance until she was 30. 'I met John, the man who was ultimately to become my husband. He was twelve years older than me and married, but had a legal separation. He didn't have any children and also said he didn't want any. We met on a church ramble. He was a gentle person, not the kind of man who would make you feel fearful. At the time he was working temporarily in north London at a radio factory. He was a musician and his orchestra had gone abroad for the summer, but didn't take everyone.' They met in 1953 but their unusual situation meant that they didn't marry until 1989. 'I suppose it was unconventional, but I didn't stop to compare it with other people's experiences. His wife was alive until 1982 and she didn't believe in divorce. John and I didn't see any reason why we should get married. We each had our own household and didn't want children. We always took holidays together and saw each other every weekend.' She says that the fact they didn't marry relieved her of the pressure to have children. 'It was a good enough reason at the time. It wouldn't be the same today, but it would have been very difficult then.' Lucy, who is now widowed, only married John for practical reasons when he became terminally ill. 'I would have some say as far as doctors were concerned in providing a home for him.'

Coral enjoys her long-distance relationship. 'When I met him he was living over here as a journalist, then he went back to Africa. He maintained the other day that he asked me to go with him, but I claim he never did. If he had asked me directly I would probably have said no. His job is now such that he spends most of his life travelling, and I probably see more of him sitting here in

London than I would if I'd gone to Africa.' She sees him once a month for three days to one week, and they have never lived together. 'That suits me very well. I'm probably better at long-distance relationships. If we had lived together we would have killed each other because we are so entirely different. We'd disagree about everything, from mundane matters such as furniture (he's the if you've got it, flaunt it variety, and I'm the understated, soft colours variety). We're both very interested in politics, which is one of the reasons why I like him, but we have different opinions. Basically we're both used to being independent and having our own way, and we both want to be boss. The last time we went on holiday together we fell out because we wanted to do different things. It allows me to get on with my life and see my friends. I think I'm better off not being married.' What holds the relationship together? 'I'm fond of him, he makes me laugh and I admire him. He comes from a background of absolutely nothing and has educated himself and now earns a lot of money. He never sits still and constantly wants to learn new things, which I find invigorating.'

Jo has been married for fifteen years, but she and her husband live in separate homes and have separate finances. 'I feel I get the benefits of being "single" by having my own home and time for myself, but also the benefits of having a partner who I see three or four times a week.'

Josephine, 63, essentially married her Italian husband so that the Home Office would let him remain in Britain, although they were also in love. She was 23 and left him in her late forties, in some doubt as to whether children would have saved the marriage or added to its difficulties. 'I got into higher education and went off to do a degree.

178

The marriage wasn't working, and I suppose it occurred to me that if we had children it might have worked. It might have given us a bond and made us like a stable, ordinary, normal marriage. We neither of us liked married life and each felt a bit tied into it, which probably means we would have felt more tied if there had been a child. My husband was shattered and surprised when I left. I suppose it took a lot of courage to move; it would have been easier to have met someone else, which is what a lot of women tend to do. It wasn't like that. It was the situation I didn't like, it would have been the same with another man. I wanted to be on my own, and loved it.' Some years later Josephine moved into the same south London house as her husband, but lived in a separate flat. 'He decided he wanted to move when he retired and I wanted a flat with a garden so we bought a house and converted it into two flats. We're on good terms and see each other from time to time. I think of him as my ex-husband. I suppose it's an unusual situation, but it seems to work.'

A few of the women enjoy sexual relationships with both men and women, and even more were open to the idea that a sexual relationship with someone of the same sex could be a possibility. 'Sexuality is not something I have strong ethical feelings about,' explains Dianne. 'I've had very important relationships with men and women. It's very easy to assume that relationships with women are going to be wonderful because they're going to under-stand you and be kind and nurturing; that can be true. I think my relationships with women have been more demanding because you expect more from them, more empathy. It's very easy to fall into the trap of thinking relationships with women are going to be great.' Dianne

179

had her first lesbian relationship eight years ago when she was 20. Her first experience was in a close relationship which developed into a sexual one. 'It seemed a perfectly natural and nice thing to do. At the time I put it down as a one-off, but in the last few years I've become more confident about my sexuality.'

Ruth, 56 and widowed, only recently started to consider that she might be bisexual, after having been married for most of her life. 'I haven't been to bed with a woman, but there are women I have close friendships with and I do know women who are lesbians,' she says. 'I feel I could perhaps go that way if the occasion arose. I wouldn't say no, definitely not.'

Penny, 30, now describes herself as a lesbian, though she had positive sexual relationships with men in her early twenties. 'Physically I'm much more attracted to women,' she says. 'Also emotionally it's far closer. Sometimes I feel like men are a different species, although there are some gay men I get along well with.' She and her long-term girlfriend have considered having a baby together by artificial insemination, and have even discussed the possibility of co-parenting with a gay male friend. 'I think the idea is romantic in theory, but in practice it would be a disaster. None of our relationships is stable enough, and it wouldn't be fair on the child. It would be far too complicated, and besides, at the moment I'm quite content with life as it is without children.'

Lack of desire to have children allows a woman a more flexible approach to her sexuality and enables her to move more freely between partners. Controversially, some women believe that it's against human nature to stay with one person throughout life, and that sexuality drives us to seek out different partners. This is certainly one established line of biological argument, based on the study of animal behaviour and the need to perpetuate genes. But anthropologists argue that sexuality in different cultures is too varied to sustain such theories. Some psychologists prefer social explanations for sexual behaviour. 'Although biological arguments can sometimes give quite a plausible account of how we might have come to behave as we do in the first place, they rarely do justice to the subtle social pressures which have come to influence our behaviour as society has evolved,' says psychologist John Nicholson.[4]

Among the interviewees are women who enjoy sexual variation and believe in serial monogamy. 'I've moved from relationship to relationship. I'm really addicted to men, I love them. I like to flirt and seduce men and conquer. I think it's a kind of addiction,' says 44-year-old Marie. Says Dianne, 28: 'I think people now aren't in one relationship for life: they're in a series of long-term relationships. Most of my relationships have lasted six months to a year, which is OK. It means I can do what I want to do and part of me doesn't want to lose that independence.' Serial monogamy has become a popular concept, especially for the 'me generation' who stresses the importance of independence, self-actualisation and personal growth, valuing constant emotional development and the inherent risk of growing out of relationships which goes with it.

Not having children may make it easier for a woman to leave a relationship. Feeling trapped in an unhappy marriage was a great fear for many women, and one of the reasons why they prefer to be child-free. Some looked at their mothers and saw them suffering an unhappy marriage for their children's sake. Some saw marital relationships as far too risky for the huge commitment of having children. 'I didn't want to be stuck with a man; with a child you are linked to him,' explains Marie, 44 and divorced. 'My ex-husband and I have a sense of duty and I think you don't divorce with children. I'm sorry, I'm very old-fashioned in a way. It's a terrible responsibility to bring a child into the world.' She was right to be cautious about her marriage: her husband left her for another woman. 'Of course I was devastated, but I'm an optimist. Every time a boyfriend or husband leaves me, I think: OK, the next one. There are so many wonderful men in the world.'

Being single

Never before in history has it been possible for so many people to remain single and live alone. According to anthropologist Helen E. Fisher, in her American best-seller, *Anatomy of Love*, divorce, marriage, remarriage, adultery, women earners and single parents are not new – but living alone is. She argues that in past centuries people had to pair up in order to farm, build shelters and protect themselves. Journalist and author Liz Hodgkinson, an advocate of the single way of life, has written a book, *Happy to be Single*.[5] 'When there was no genuine alternative, when women couldn't earn a living, and subsistence economies meant that men and women had to form lifelong paired units, there was some point in turning a necessity into a virtue and pretending there was something holy and wonderful about coupling up for life. Now that there is no longer any need to elevate marriage and monogamy as a sacrament, perhaps we should begin to see it for the empty illusion it is,' says Hodgkinson.[6] 'Nowadays, it's the single people who can truly have it all – friendship, love, career, money, an active social life – without having to carry around the baggage of a permanent partner.'

At present 16 per cent of British woman in their thirties are single, and more people are living alone, whether through choice or circumstances: a quarter of households in Britain consist of one person. Despite the increase in single women, the word spinster is still feared, conjuring up images of the haggard elderly woman who is too unattractive or uninteresting to ensnare a man. The term derives from 'woman who spins', a common female occupation in the last century. Unmarried women were rife during the Victorian period: one in four didn't marry because of the lack of men caused by soldiering, war casualties and emigration. Known as 'old maids', they were considered a serious social problem.

Although increasingly accepted and popular, the single life certainly isn't for everyone, and the high rates of remarriage are a testament to the desirability of partner-ship, despite its difficulties and personal sacrifices. Lonely-heart columns are in abundance, and the match-making agency Dateline registers 3,000 new members a month. However, men seem to benefit more than women from married life. Single men are more likely than married ones to suffer depression, and they also top the charts for suicides. Married women are more likely than single men to suffer anxiety and depression: they report levels that are two to three times higher than those of their single counterparts. Additionally women's emotional adjustment to divorce is superior to that of men's. One could conclude that women put more labour into marriage than men, and men receive more servicing and support. Another key factor for women's mental health is employment outside the home, which contributes enormously to women's sense of wellbeing.

'I'm happy being single,' states Sue, 33, a woman with a stimulating job as a journalist, an attractive London flat and busy social life. She arrived at this conclusion after a painful voyage of self-discovery and politicisation. Previously, she lived with a partner for five years. 'I was cooking the meals, doing the shopping, sewing his buttons on, and I gradually became very disenchanted with this. It seemed I was doing these things because he was anxious about his career and I should support him in this. It suddenly dawned on me: why was I doing all this? Why didn't I work on my career? Why did I have to do all the cleaning and shopping? Why was he so hopeless? Suddenly the personal was political and I became a feminist overnight.' After the break-up of her relationship she became involved in a destructive *ménage à trois*: her new partner had an out-of-town long-term girlfriend. The trauma of this took her into psychotherapy for four years, a very rewarding and positive experience: 'I had all these insights into myself and came to realise I was caught up in this dreadful chain because of my lack of self-esteem, and felt I didn't deserve a man, only half a man. Through therapy I was able to disentangle myself and be on my own which was terribly liberating. From thinking that being on your own was really sad, somehow you were a failure, I suddenly found it was quite nice. I have all my own space and can do whatever I like.' Since finishing therapy she has been casually dating. 'I'm lightly trawling, but I don't feel I need a man,' she says. As Sue doesn't want children, she doesn't feel pressurised by her biological clock to meet the right partner quickly.

Likewise Trudy, 31, a catering manager, who divorced after six years of marriage says she prefers being single. 'Maybe I had a bad marriage and everything else, but it is the sense of freedom, not being dependent on a man to do things for you. I save really hard to go on nice holidays. The rest of the time I spend doing my garden. I go out, go for walks. If the overtime comes I can say yes without having to confer with anyone. If I want to go to a night-club I go with my Saturday staff, or we'll go down the pub and have a laugh and joke, but at the end of the evening I'm glad to get home and be on my own.' She admits that there are drawbacks, 'when it's a rainy Sunday and you're stuck indoors and have done everything you can do'.

Ruth, 56, has been a widow for the past ten years, and although not euphoric about being single, is content with the situation. 'Occasionally, I think it would be nice to meet the right partner,' she muses. 'I've got a man friend I go on holiday with, not a sex man friend, very good pals and that's nice. I've got close male friends and female friends and I think that's probably all I want.'

Katrin, 27, has never had a long-term relationship, and feels she would quite like one. 'I started with a married man to make sure that it didn't come too close, and then this summer I thought, why not? I like men. I quite like to be alone, but I'd like to be in a relationship,' she says. 'Marriage isn't important to me at all. Maybe the divorce of my parents has something to do with it.' Although she is not seeking a partner so that she can have children, she is open to the idea that she might change her mind should her partner strongly want to be a father. 'It's difficult, but I think I would start to think about it again.'

7

WORK AND THE LEISURE LIFESTYLE

Women at work is not new: in pre-industrial times both men and women worked for the family subsistence. With industrialisation a woman's working place became defined as the home, a pattern that was seen as a reflection of the natural order of sexual division of labour. A hundred years ago a woman's career choice was very limited: she could become a nurse, typist, teacher, or doctor if she could get a place in one of the very few medical schools which admitted women, but she could not become a lawyer or join the higher ranks of the civil service.

Two world wars were the catalyst that changed for ever how women were viewed in the workplace. Their employment became a necessity during the First World War when, for the first time, women could prove their abilities in jobs that had traditionally been reserved for men. It is estimated that 400,000 domestic servants downed their buckets and brushes to work in factories. They also worked on the railways and buses, and some middle-class women drove ambulances and nursed. Between the wars women had to retreat to the domestic sphere because of male unemployment. In some professions, teaching for example, there was even a 'marriage bar' which meant that women had to leave their jobs when they married.

Despite this return to traditional roles, the war had irrevocably changed the concept of women at home, and with the advent of the Second World War they returned *en masse* to the factories and farms. However, it took until 1975 for women to win the legal right to equal pay and rights in the workplace, and the struggle continues today. Women still disproportionately dominate lower-paid jobs: typists and secretaries are 98 per cent female and shop assistants 84 per cent; whereas only 2 per cent of women are surgeons and only 15 per cent solicitors. Women are also less likely to be promoted. 'Sometimes it's blatant discrimination,' says Jill Chesworth of the Equal Opportunities Commission. 'Women are discriminated against because they take breaks in the work market or work part-time. Women's skills are valued less, and employers don't think that they're up to the job. We find such cases very hard to prove and only win one case in four.'

Just one generation ago women did not necessarily expect to have a working life outside the home. The mothers of women like Elizabeth, Helen and Janet would probably speak very differently about the importance of a career in their lives. Many younger women look back at their mothers' lives and see them as having been trapped in relationships of dependence because of the lack of employment opportunities. 'Work is very important to me. I never wanted to be like my mother who didn't have a job and seemed to have so few options,' says Marnie, 31, who works as a teacher. 'She couldn't have left my father even if she hated him, because there was no way out. Maybe it's a basic lack of trust: I'm willing to throw everything into work, but I'm very wary of giving up things for other people. They can never be relied upon. This is my flat, not my boyfriend's.' Marnie's mother is unlikely to have been given the type of educational literature which today is published by the Equal Opportunities Commission. Schoolgirls are urged to think seriously about their future careers. 'Work is not just something done between leaving school and having babies. Choice of career and earning capacity can make a big difference to the quality of life,' it reads. Attitudes have changed very quickly and the depth of the revolution is reflected in a recent MORI poll which revealed that only one in five Britons now believes that a woman's place is in the home.

Women want quality work: they like it. Studies repeatedly show that paid employment outside the home is beneficial to women's sense of well-being, offering financial independence, stimulation, a sense of self-worth, companionship and more. 'It's one of the most important things in my life. It's an obsession, it's what I live for. I'm completely dedicated and love every minute of it. It's different every day and there are always new challenges. I come into contact with a lot of people and I get great joy in getting someone an interview that leads to a job. It's definitely going to be part of my life until I retire,' enthuses Elizabeth, 26, a theatrical agent. 'I couldn't conceive not having a job. Although I'm married I still want to be independent and in control,' says Helen, 26, a medical support worker. 'The two most important things

188

to me about my work are the independence I get from it, and the chance to use my brain and be constantly learning. I need to keep my mind active, and not get into a rut, and to feel that I'm doing socially useful work. I also need to know that I'm earning my own money, to do more or less as I please with, and not to be financially dependent on my husband or anyone else,' says Janet, 29, who combines working part-time in a library with studying for a degree.

Having children is creative: it is about engaging in the world, having an impact, achieving, doing, leaving a mark, realising your potential. Until the career ladder became available to women, bearing and raising children was often the only way women could move through time purposefully, find narrative and meaning in their lives. Yet history is punctuated with remarkable women who stepped outside convention in order to lead extraordinary working lives. Philosophers, artists, writers, travellers, political activists, nuns, nurses and doctors all rank amongst the child-free women who make up our heritage. But these women have been the exceptions, drawn away from motherhood by their talents. Now ordinary women too have a choice: fecundity no longer has to take centre stage. 'I always felt I wanted to change things and have an effect. I've got a social conscience. My father was in the Labour party and very staunch. I need to be doing something useful, where I can make small bits of progress and see things happening,' says Dianne, 28, talking passionately about her job as a charity press officer.

What is clear is that in the current job market work and motherhood often militate against each other. Again and again, surveys and studies highlight how strained women feel when trying to juggle the two. According to a

189

1992 Gallup survey, 90 per cent of mothers in paid employment have difficulty balancing their roles and face both practical and emotional difficulties. The most common problem is the lack of time for themselves, and the fact that most still have to do the housework – the 'second shift', as it has become known. Other problems are the high cost of childcare and inadequate facilities, feelings of guilt about leaving a child, lack of promotion, inflexible working hours and lack of understanding from partners. When asked what qualities working parents need, the women replied, 'the stamina of a long-distance runner'.

For most women having a baby means having less money – considerably less. According to a report from the Family Policy Studies Centre *Babies and Money*, 1986, the estimated cost to a 'typical' woman who leaves her £7,000 yearly job to have two children is £135,000. This takes into account her loss of earnings due to short hours, lower rates of pay and time away from paid employment. While the direct cost of having a baby is about £30,000 for the child's first sixteen years, the cost to the mother in lost pay is much higher. The Equal Opportunities Commission estimates that having children can cost women up to half of their lifetime's earnings. An estimate from a survey commissioned by the life assurance company, Equity and Law, puts the cost of having a child at £122,675 from birth to 21 years.[1] Women are starting to question this inordinately high price. 'Who needs babies?' asks one headline in the *Evening Standard* (June 1993) in a feature by Jill Tweedie.

As I lie in bed on a Sunday morning, one thing in life becomes even more surprising. Why on earth, in this post-Pill age, do so many women have children? Perhaps some do because they haven't much else – no training, no money, no job. Even so, kids only add to their burdens: you can see that in any supermarket queue. But how about the women who have everything – education, ambition, careers, prospects, freedom to do whatever they like? What makes them act like lemmings, chucking themselves in droves off the panoramic headland onto the rocks below?

Children or career

A recent survey of 1,000 women carried out for the National Council of Women of Great Britain showed that for nearly 80 per cent of women under 35, getting on in a job was more important than having children.[2] Among women of childbearing age, few believed they needed a child or a stable relationship to feel fulfilled. It is apparent that in recent years career aspirations have become extremely important for women, but from the fifty women I spoke with, it is largely untrue to say that a woman doesn't want children solely because she prefers to have a career, although this is popularly thought to be the explanation for women's child-free status. There is a fast-growing stereotype of the ageing career woman, lonely, bitter and unfulfilled because she has missed out on motherhood. She is spiteful and jealous of younger female colleagues, may hit the bottle during those lonely evenings, and preys on the blood of younger men. It's a powerful image, but where does it come from? It should be remembered that throughout the ages any woman who has chosen to live her life unconventionally, sidestepping male authority, has come in for aggressive stereotyping:

feminists have been cartooned as dykes in dungarees; divorced women labelled 'loose' or neurotic; unmarried women are shrivelled up spinsters, and single elderly women living alone were witches. Motherhood continues to be viewed as the superior and 'natural' role. 'Work is unfortunately still cast in second-best terms for female identity, and not viewed as a coequal option to mother-hood. That it is becoming increasingly acceptable for women to find fulfilment in nonmaternal occupations does not seen to have substantially altered the underlying belief that these alternatives are substitutes for women's real purpose and source of personal fulfilment,' writes psychologist Mardy Ireland in *Reconceiving Women: Separating Motherhood from Female Identity*.[3]

Career considerations certainly reinforce a woman's decision not to have children, but the means by which this decision is reached are enormously emotional and complex: the spectre of the boardroom chair is just one aspect of many. As one woman said: 'If I'd wanted children that much I would have had them and somehow managed. The truth is I didn't want them that much anyway.' Women like Karen know that it would prove very difficult to combine work with motherhood. Karen cites two pregnant women who are about to leave her orchestra because of the impossibility. 'Music and motherhood just don't combine, it's absolutely disastrous,' she says. 'Last year we did three weeks in the States, and a week around Europe. When I'm performing God knows what time I get to bed.' Karen adores her work, she has wanted to be a professional musician since the age of 18 when she joined a youth orchestra. 'I enjoy making music, being in this team of people giving enjoyment to other people, to be part of this whole performance, to communicate something – it fills me. I enjoy the fact that we get paid to go and see all these interesting countries. It's a daily challenge to sustain the standard and that stimulates me.' When asked why she doesn't want children Karen doesn't even mention her career, but talks emotionally about the fact that her mother died of cancer when she was seven and that she believes that 'I have always had a subconscious desire not to repeat that pattern and inflict on a young child the emotional trauma of losing a mother.' She has also watched her older sister coping with early motherhood and saw it as a role 'fraught with frustrations. I watched all this and thought "I must make sure I don't make those mistakes." ' Karen chose to marry a man who was clear in his intent not to have children, and thereafter her decision was 'straightforward'.

A group of woman for whom work was not of much importance further reinforce the notion that women do not choose to forgo motherhood simply because of their career aspirations. Sally, 32, works as a customer service adviser for a building society. Previously she ran a newsagency, but gave it up because she found it too stressful. 'I thought it's not worth it, so I sold up and went for this job. I wouldn't describe myself as a career person. I would quite enjoy just working in a small shop. Having a career is not why I don't want a family. It's more comfortable for people to think it's because you want a career. There's a friend at work who says she doesn't want children because she wants a house and holidays. But that's not why I don't want children. I just don't want children.'

The interviewees were by no means all high-flyers: one works part-time in a clothes shop, another is a caretaker for a block of flats, there's an office temp, a factory worker and one who described herself as a housewife. Some say that they 'just have a job for the money', but most view their work as important in a variety of ways. Pauline, 50, the caretaker, says, 'It's nice to know you are valued for what you do and I enjoy mixing with people'. Carolyn, 44, who works in a clothes shop, says, 'I like meeting people and keeping up with the latest fashion trends. I also like the independence my wages give me.'

Workplace discrimination

Keeping women in unsatisfying dead-end jobs has been one of the ways society has encouraged women to have children. To a woman who is stuck in a boring job with little chance of promotion, motherhood must look a more creative and interesting way to spend her life. Janette, 30, works as a legal secretary, a job which is well paid but one she finds dull. 'I've done it for fifteen years, and it's the same thing day in and day out. I only stay there for the money,' she says. 'I'd much rather do something different. At school I wanted to be a dentist, but biology was so difficult it made me change my mind. Mum enrolled me in a secretarial college, which I was pleased about at the time.'

The tedium of the job has made her think about motherhood as an escape, and at one point she put herself in the hands of fate by coming off the pill for three months. 'I was just bored with work and looking for a change.' Her situation is very different to that of university-educated Sue, who works as a journalist for an entertainment magazine. 'It's 90 per cent of my life. It's a have-fun job. I'm out every night reviewing films or plays, and I never get really tired of that. I love going to the theatre and eating in expensive restaurants, and going to the movies. It's a dream! Why would I give that up to come home and sit with a baby?'

Even though we have equal opportunity in theory, in practice the workplace still operates to oust women and get them back to those prams. Women who are pregnant can find themselves made 'redundant' or suddenly fired on false pretences. It is difficult to give an exact figure of the number of dismissals of pregnant women each year, as most cases never reach a tribunal. This is mainly because if a woman has not worked for at least two years, she cannot use the unfair dismissal laws. A recent survey, *Maternity Rights in Britain* by the Policy Studies Institute, found that 53 per cent of women were in employment when their pregnancy began, but that 7 per cent of these lost their jobs or had to stop work earlier than they had intended.[4] One in seven of those who lost their jobs had actually been dismissed. This could mean that as many as 3,500 women a year face dismissal, with a further 21,000 stopping work before they intended to. Unskilled or semi-skilled workers are most at risk: Paula McQuaide had been working as a waitress for five months when she told her employer she was pregnant. Shortly afterwards she was off sick for a few days and on her return was dismissed with a week's notice. A tribunal upheld her discrimination complaint, and she was awarded £2,026 compensation.

If women do manage to retain their jobs when they become mothers, they then confront the increased likelihood that they will not be promoted. Men do not face the same problem when they become fathers: probably quite the reverse. Men with families are seen to be stable and hard-working, good for the company image and eminently

195

promotable. A survey published by the Institute of Manpower Studies[5] discovered that professional and managerial women who return to work after having a baby believe their career prospects have been harmed. The report concluded that 60 per cent of 785 women interviewed had lower employment prospects despite mothers returning to work earlier and in greater numbers after having children. Wendy Hirsh, one of the authors of the report, says that women 'feel their career has to take a back seat and that managers see them as less promotable once they have become mothers'.

Many of the interviewees were acutely aware of the tension between career aspirations and motherhood. 'I think it's inevitable that being child-free will affect my future prospects. I will be able to decide how much time and energy I want to give to my career without having to weigh up the needs of children against it, and will not have to interrupt my career midstream to raise them,' says Janet, 29, and married, who worked as a secretary but has gone back to university as a mature student to study social science. 'If we'd been supporting one or more dependent children, I doubt I would have had the time, energy or money to return to university.'

Trudy, 31, a catering manager in charge of a 110-seat restaurant in a high street store, says she watches her sister-in-law who is also in catering and has three children. 'She tries to keep on a level with me, but is always having to adjust it so that she can be home for the children. I'll have better prospects because I'll be free to put myself forward. I want to get on in catering. I'd like to go as high as possible: I wouldn't mind being a small hotel manager, then a general manager of a big hotel complex.'

Ruth, 56, an engineer, says, 'It would have been more difficult with children to have got as much promotion as I did. Occasionally my work involves going away from home and late-night meetings.' A male-dominated environment, engineering does not easily accommodate the needs of women with children, and Ruth has felt prejudice against women amongst 'the old guard', but expresses optimism that younger men are more welcoming.

Tanujah, currently employed as a youth worker, hopes to retrain to be a nurse. Eventually she hopes to work abroad, and believes that this might be incompatible with a family life. 'I'd like to work in the developing world – Africa or Bangladesh. My main ambition is to have a job that's fulfilling, that gives me a better understanding of the world we live in.'

The public sector is generally more supportive of working mothers and led the way in the 1980s with imaginative innovations, such as job sharing and career breaks, to help women continue working during the child-bearing and childrearing years. Those child-free women working in the public sector said that it would not be impossible for them to combine employment with the responsibilities of children. 'I'm reliably assured it isn't that difficult to have children in the civil service. A pregnant colleague has been informed it's fine to take off as much maternity leave as necessary. Another woman has gone part time because of her children. It's very good for working mothers: you can take five years as a career break and come back in the same grade,' says Amelia, a 22-year-old graduate in the civil service fast stream. She still believes, however, that she will be advantaged by not having children because she will not have to delay any part of her career, although she worries that male colleagues will prove hostile to a woman who does not want motherhood. 'I don't know yet whether senior male managers will think there's "something wrong" with me. The civil service is still very male dominated in the top rank,' she says.

Jill, a 26-year-old teacher, also feels that behind closed doors there is prejudice in the public sector. 'I've been in that bracket where it's will she or won't she? The management aren't saying it, but you know it's going through their minds. I just know them: that's how they talk about other women. You know, they've got one eye on the clock: will she be around next year? The head tends to promote the younger teacher or the older teacher. We're only a small school and it's been quite disruptive in the past few years.' Jill, who is married, had never talked openly with her employers about not wanting children, but her situation is now clear following a recent hysterectomy.' 'I think my promotion prospects have improved,' she says.

Recently much attention has been paid to 'women returners' following a government initiative which tried to tempt more mothers back to the workplace, as part of Opportunity 2000, a campaign to promote women at work. According to the Central Statistical Office's Social Trends, about 40 per cent of women currently return to employment before their children are five. The concern over women returners has been motivated by demographics: a drop in the number of young people entering the workforce in the 1980s was expected to lead to shortfalls in employees. By 2001 it is estimated that there will be nearly a million fewer young people under the age of 25. It was hoped that mothers could make up the numbers, although as the recession took hold, redundancy rather than recruitment has dictated employment policy.

Women face many problems when they take extended breaks from their careers: lack of self-confidence is the stumbling block most frequently cited. Many feel that they no longer have skills to offer and that business life has moved on and left them behind. The Women Returners' Network (WRN) is a charity set up in 1984 to promote education, training and employment opportunities for mothers wanting to return to employment. It publishes a national directory featuring thousands of courses for women returners, and estimates that one-third of women with dependent children are working or seeking work. 'In a recent survey in Europe flexible working time was found to be the most significant factor in attracting them to the employer,' says a spokeswoman for WRN. 'It was more important than anything else, including workplace nurseries, of which we have hardly any anyway. Flexible working time is the crux of it.'

Overwhelmingly what women need is a working environment which is more 'family-friendly', a word that is about to enter the corporate vocabulary. Career breaks, flexi-hours, job shares and workplace nurseries, plus an equal share in childraising from men, are top of the agenda. When looking at the problem of managing work and family life, the emphasis is always placed on women's working conditions, but the biggest revolution needs to be in employment that is traditionally male dominated. British men work the longest hours in Europe, making it impossible for them to take equal responsibility for their children. Few companies would be sympathetic to a man taking the afternoon off to take his children to the dentist or attend a school play. Some organisations are calling for government policy to ensure family-friendly working: statutory leave to care for sick children, better maternity and paternity leave. Unfortunately, the needs of profit-making companies are not always in accordance with the needs of families, yet it is the families who make up the consumers which sustain their business. Women as consumers are a powerful force, and it is no coincidence that the companies which have been most family friendly are those which rely heavily on female patronage.

Hopefully working conditions will change with time, and women will not feel that their need to have children is so incompatible with their need to be in a paid employment. Until that day, career aspirations significantly support and feed the decision-making process about being child-free.

A new self-identity

Women's struggle to enter the workforce is about more than the right to earn a living. It is also about the right to seek a sense of self beyond family relationships. As mothers and wives, women have long sacrificed self-interest in devotion to husbands and children. 'We weren't desperately poor, but if there were only three chops my mum would go without and have a piece of cheese,' remembers Helen, 26. 'We came first. She never had nice clothes when we were growing up and was dreadfully dowdy. My mum has nice clothes now and good taste: I can see what a sacrifice it would have been to her.'

Essentially in a weak and dependent position, women found that to assert their needs and demands they had to

200

wriggle through the gaps, manipulate if necessary, take a seat at the table by coming through the back door. Often women have used their role as family martyr to powerful effect: guilt and love are a potent combination. Helen says that her mother used her martyrdom as 'a tool against us. She always said she had done her best for me and I was being ungrateful.' Then along came the feminist movement with its assertion that women should acknowledge their needs. Women's self-assertion classes became popular nationwide, a ubiquitous part of adult education programmes. Here women were encouraged to ask for what they want, directly and assertively.

This has gone hand in hand with the 'me generation'. It's a term that comes from writer Tom Wolfe, and describes the young who grew up in the 1960s and 1970s, two decades of social change. This period marked the emergence of the hippie counterculture and stressed individualism, 'doing your own thing' and hedonism, 'if it feels good do it'. The optimism that human nature is essentially good was romantically embodied by the image of the 'flower children'.

The 'me generation' were brought up by parents who valued family life highly, often putting children's needs and wishes first at great sacrifice. Consequently they have grown up with a strong sense of self-worth and stress the value of inner exploration, 'wholeness' and the pursuit of individual happiness.

During these decades new humanistic therapies evolved: Gestalt therapy, encounter groups, body-orientated techniques developed by Wilhelm Reich, and transpersonal psychology. Psychotherapy and counselling centres report that the numbers of people going into therapy (and training to become therapists) have now reached record levels. Individual therapies, groups and classes have proved very popular among the middle classes, and a number of the interviewees had taken part in such activities. Women who don't specifically subscribe to 'humanistic' ideologies have been influenced by these views: self-help, personal growth and recovery features are a staple of the women's magazine market; popular psychology books are a growth market. Humanistic psychology spills into the New Age movement where it takes on spiritual dimensions that have proved popular with those who have grown disillusioned with institutionalised religions.

Writer Judith D. Schwartz sees the 'human potential movement' as having filled a 'void' left when feminism withdrew from motherhood, as women looked around for an alternative sense of status and self-esteem: 'By the time people got around to having children, many were undoubtedly too wearied by the task of raising themselves to think about raising anyone else.'⁶ Whether the movement filled a 'void' or usefully created a new space is debatable, but combined with feminism the two had a powerful impact on women, reassuring them that it was all right to put themselves at the centre of their lives and find meaning in life outside of the sacrificial role of mother. They have given women the freedom to explore themselves, whereas previously they had always been defined by their relationships to men. A girl is the daughter of her father the banker, train driver, judge. The woman is the wife of her husband, the banker, train driver, judge. It has not been easy for a woman to take on the concept that she is free to define herself. 'We give up something, a special privilege wound up in the culture-laden word "mother" which we will not instantly regain in the form of freedom and power,' writes Ann Snitow in *Feminist Review*.[7] It is difficult for a woman to let go of that legacy of thought which tells her to play the martyred mother and rewards her for doing so. Mothers may be second-class citizens in a practical sense, but spiritually they are eulogised: a mother's selflessness has traditionally been her source of pride and self-value. A woman defining herself for herself is consequently fraught with conflict, terrified on the one hand that she is being selfish, terrified on the other that she is being weak, subservient and untrue to herself.

This tension is reflected in the frequent accusation that child-free women are selfish, as if women have a social obligation to produce children. Perhaps this could have been argued to be true when populations dwindled miserably because of the ravages of disease and war, but any quick assessment of the problems of overpopulation should be adequate reassurance that women have a social responsibility to restrain their fertility. Yet child-free women are still accused of being selfish, and likewise accuse themselves. 'It's true, I am selfish,' declares Liz, 40, who has chosen not to have children because 'babies leave me cold and I value my independence very much. I do not have to make any decisions in my life on the basis of how it would affect a family.' Says Helen, 26: 'It upsets me when I'm accused of being selfish, but I half believe it.'

There is a popular notion that women who choose not to have children are more materialistic, opting for the spurious consumer pleasures in preference to the love and nurturing of a baby. 'The common view of the child-free is that they are self-centred, materialistic people who don't want children because they would interfere with their own hedonistic lifestyles. I have never understood why the mere fact that someone is uninterested in being personally involved in the bearing and raising of children is taken to mean that they are also incapable of being caring, generous, dedicated, or of making any significant contribution to the happiness and welfare of others,' argues Janet, 29.

Money was rarely cited by the interviewees as a reason for not having children. If money was an issue, it centred primarily on the fear of poverty rather than the desire for wealth. 'I want to have enough money for my husband and I not to have to worry about paying the bills,' says Helen, 26. 'As far as the financial aspect goes, being child-free hasn't meant that I can afford a luxurious lifestyle. Fat chance on £140 per week. Many parents prefer to spend money on cigarettes and booze rather than on their children,' says Julia, 32, a foundry worker. 'I don't want to be poor again,' says Miriam, 33, who suffered crippling debts when she and her husband first bought their home. She points out that being child-free means she can afford to stay in her job as an AIDS researcher, instead of having to find higher-paid work which she might not find as satisfying. Other women too argued that being child-free liberated them from materialism and the necessity to earn high salaries and to have to afford child-minders. Penny, 30, can afford to work just a four-day week as a graphic designer, and freely gives her remaining day to a gay women's voluntary organisation.

Many of the women argued that it is people who choose to have children who are the selfish ones:

It doesn't make sense: if you want children surely that is selfish as you are doing something for yourself. (Charlotte, 34)

204

I feel many people are selfish to have a child if circumstances are against a child being happily brought up or the child was not planned. (Julia, 32)

My husband and I have given a great deal of thought to the business of procreation. Do potential parents think about the life they are creating purely for the child's sake and not from their self-fulfilment point of view? Now who are the selfish ones? (Karen, 36)

Isn't it selfish to have them when you are not sure, or for the wrong reason? (Terri, 33)

I don't think people ask themselves why they have children. There are a lot of children who are abused and unhappy. I think people have children too easily and that's bloody selfish. Maybe you don't really want them, or are not financially secure, or don't have time to spend with them, or are with a violent partner. (Dianne, 28)

Women with children are selfish in overpopulating the world, and in always expecting other people to cope with their children and overlook their bad behaviour, like running about in restaurants and spoiling other diners' meals. Also they expect their children to look after them in old age: they are selfishly too dependent on their own children. (Rose, 42)

Other women had confidently taken on board the philosophies of feminism and individualism and asserted it as their right to be emphatic about their own personal needs:

What is wrong with being selfish? And what is so unselfish about having a child? The world would be a better place if all women were a bit more selfish and chose what is right for them. (Jo, 39)

If you juggle work with having a child where would be the free time for yourself, what I call dreamtime? Just reflecting about your own life. Women feel they're selfish if they do it. No! All of them should do it. (Marie, 44)

Women have bent over backwards for other people long enough. It's time we stood up and started thinking about what we want for a change. That's not selfish, only fair and right. (Penny, 30)

I think women aren't selfish enough. (Maria, 29)

The leisure-centred lifestyle

Leisure time is growing, and with it the idea that pleasure is a valuable human experience. In the late 1920s the length of the working day and week began to diminish, leading to an increasing interest in spare-time activities. Women have been particularly liberated by the development of labour- and time-saving devices in the home. Earlier retirement and longer life expectancy have also contributed to the trend, as have redundancies in the 1990s. Some sociologists argue that leisure time has existed in all civilisations, and others that it really came into being with the industrial revolution when the workplace became clearly separated from the home. It is certainly true that in earlier times leisure used to be synonymous with religious festivities, and the liturgical calendar remains the way our secular culture defines much of its leisure time: Christmas and Easter are major national holidays, although few engage in the religious rituals on which they are centred.

Hobbies and free time were enormously important for the child-free women and the list of activities they take part in was vast: horse-riding, writing, volunteer work, rock-climbing, sailing, circle-dancing, dressmaking, fine art, adult education, rambling and socialising, to mention but a few. For some women hobbies and free time were much more important than their employment, and formed the focus of their life. 'My ambitions are directed towards my hobbies. I'm doing my honours for an Open University degree. I'm interested in volcanoes and have climbed four active volcanoes helping the OU people doing measurements. I'm the secretary for my local Open University geological society and do all the newsletters,' says Miriam, 33.

Jane, 29, goes through the breathless weekly schedule of leisure pursuits she and her husband enjoy: 'to run through a week: we're both working full-time, I'm out Monday and Tuesday nights at the poly. Alex has guitar lessons Monday night. A few Wednesdays of the month we go to local bike meetings. Thursdays I do voluntary work for a local cat rescue: I drive around all night picking up and depositing cats. Alex is at college Thursday. Friday night I spend in the library. Weekends are generally spent running around the supermarket. On Sunday in the summer we go to a lot of Volkswagen events because we like old Volkswagens and exhibit in classic car shows. I go to the gym most lunchtimes. Our house has been for sale for three years because we want to buy a narrow boat.'

Crucially, being child-free gives women the time to explore these pursuits, and freedom was a word almost

207

universally used by the interviewees when asked about the benefits of not having children. The sense of liberation is inherent in the term child-free. 'We can be our own bosses, be spontaneous, and not have to consider anyone else but ourselves,' says Louise, 34, speaking of life with her husband. 'I can come and go as I please and am not at anyone's beck and call,' says Carolyn, 44. 'I'm reluctant to give up the freedom I didn't gain until the age of 28,' says Julia, 32, who spent many years looking after her mentally ill mother who eventually committed suicide. 'We are mobile and can go where we like, when we like, and just take off when we want to, which we do quite often,' says Georgina, 32, whose vision of her leisure-based lifestyle stretches to plans for early retirement.

In research for which she interviewed 156 child-free couples, sociologist Jean Veevers likewise discovered that the concept of freedom was central to their decision not to start a family. Veevers, however, concludes that this much-talked-about freedom was more important in theory than practice:

> Although they refer to freedom often, and maintain that it is an issue of central concern, their daily round of activities does not seem substantially more free than that of many parents. Like their more conventional counterparts, most are bound by the constraints of a monogamous marriage, a nine to five job, and a limited amount of time, money and imagination. However, the childless still report that they *feel* free.[8]

I think Veevers underestimates the amount of freedom the child-free enjoy. True, most of them do not take off to walk barefoot across India, but they do benefit from an abundance of less dramatic, but equally valuable freedoms: spontaneous weekends away, a night at the pub, going for a walk on a sunny summer evening, sleeping on the settee on a Sunday afternoon, etc. Most important of all was feeling that they were potentially free should they *choose* to be so. 'It's being able to say "Do you fancy going out tonight?" or "Shall we go on holiday?" Being able to go into town after work, being able to sit and read all evening and not have to put a child to bed. It all sounds very trivial. We like going to the pub and we like dancing at a club in Sheffield. We go to the pictures. I'd love to have a car and be able to take off and go camping,' says Helen, 26.

Child-free women express enthusiasm for travel, and it was the most frequently cited ambition when asked about their dreams for the future. Marnie, 31, plans to teach in Japan; Janette, 30, and her husband are planning to travel in America; Amelia, 22 and her boyfriend want to go to Egypt; Angie, 27 wants to go back to Jamaica to visit her grandmother; Katy, 23 and her husband are looking into emigrating to New Zealand; Marion, 41, who has already spent some time living in Australia, hopes to work six months a year and travel for the rest of the time. Says Janet, 29: 'I definitely want to travel, I can't see myself ever getting enough of that.' Quite a few had a real taste for adventure and enjoyed visiting the types of places where it would be difficult to take children. 'I'm interested in going to countries like Africa. Last year I went to the Gambia, and this year I'm going to Kenya on a camping trip. I travel on my own and find it quite easy. The first time it was a goal at the end of my year when I was getting divorced. I'd already been to Morocco and Tunisia and touched the top of Africa, and I wanted to go further down the coast. Gambia was in the brochure and I thought, if I book it now I'll have something to look forward to after my divorce. I went out there and had a great time and got invited back to stay with some African people in their village. I went again last March and everyone was really friendly, and I tend to be the outgoing type. In the bar and for meals it was no hardship: I spoke to the Gambians about catering and napkin folding, things like that,' says Trudy, a catering manager.

When we say 'yes' to something, we are also saying 'no' to something else. These women are saying 'yes' to every advantage possible within their paid employment, 'yes' to finding an identity outside of the traditional family role, 'yes' to leisure time and personal freedom. What they are saying 'no' to is childbearing and childraising – a high price to pay, some mothers may think. But to the child-free all the elements of life to which they have said 'yes' are highly prized, and although some may have regrets and acknowledge ambiguities, others feel totally fulfilled. All of them would agree that what is important is that they are free to make that choice.

8

INFERTILITY

WHY write about women who *can't* have children in a book which is about women who *choose* not to have children? What can the two groups possibly have in common? First, it seems important to acknowledge that choice is a privilege that not all people enjoy and no matter how many strides forward we have made in self-determination, not everything is under our control. One in six couples suffers fertility problems. 'It's a problem that is as widespread as cancer,' says John Dickson, director of ISSUE, the national fertility association. Many of the child-free interviewees said that although they choose not to have children they would be distraught if they discovered they didn't have the option of having a family. 'I see being able to have a baby as an empowering thing. I would be quite upset if I found out I was infertile. It would mean I wasn't a woman in a way. Does that make sense? It would be like I'd had part of me taken away,' says Maria. When so much female identity rests on motherhood, the woman who does not have children through choice can at least buoy her femaleness by saying 'I could have had a child if I'd wanted one.'

Secondly, infertile women who want to become mothers have often thought long and hard about what parenthood means to them, probably more so than those who have successfully had families. No woman puts herself through painful, emotionally gruelling and often expensive fertility treatments without having first explored the reasons why she wants to have a baby. Infertile women have much to say about what it means to become a mother, and therefore what it also means *not* to become a mother. As one infertile woman emotionally puts it: 'We've got to live with this hell, because it is a living hell being childless when you haven't chosen to be childless. We've got to make sense of it; we've got to explore the maze whether we want to or not.'

Women who are unable to bear children have historically been labelled barren; a repugnant term which is now thankfully going out of usage. It is a word which suggests that a woman has no identity or value beyond her capacity to reproduce. Barren: it implies emptiness, desolation, uselessness, aridity. Although the dictionary definition does not relate it to a specific sex, the word is never used to describe an infertile man. To not be a father does not negate a man's identity in the way that not being a mother negates a woman's. For thousands of years and all over the world, fertility has been honoured, infertility shunned. Children have traditionally been the means by which couples provide for themselves in their old age. Where the home is the economic unit, more children means more hands to plough the fields and tend the

212

flocks. There is a great emphasis on fertility, especially where infant mortality is high and a woman might need to give birth to ten children if she hopes to raise seven. In *Women as Mothers* Sheila Kitzinger describes some responses to infertility worldwide:

> So great was the emphasis on fertility that in certain African tribes (the Dahomey, for example) an impotent husband urged his wife to sleep with a friend or relative, or if a wife could not bear children another woman was brought in to bear them 'to his name'. In some societies barrenness or impotence are sufficient grounds for divorce. In Tikopia, a small island in the Western Pacific, for instance, couples may separate on grounds of childlessness without any formal annulling of the marriage. In Sudanese Africa the Nuer bride does not even go to her husband's home until the first baby is weaned. There is no point in the relationship continuing unless the child survives.[1]

There is a long-held stigma associated with infertility. Women ravaged by childhood illnesses often grow up infertile, reinforcing the deep associations between infertility, death and decay. Many cultures have connected infertility with sin: if children are the gift of God, then the lack of them may be a wrathful God's way of punishing an evil woman. Germaine Greer points out that infertility is often associated with lechery and sexual sin, whilst virginity and modesty are associated with fruitfulness. She writes: 'Women who flaunt their sexuality driving men to squander their precious seed in barren wombs, are the personifications of death, disease and evil the world over.'[2]

There is a cultural belief that infertility is a female problem. This is incorrect: fertility difficulties are evenly divided between women and men – approximately 30 per cent female, 30 per cent male. In about 10 per cent of all cases of infertility, no cause can be identified; of the remaining 30 per cent infertility results from couples having a combination of problems, such as the inability of sperm to penetrate the cervical mucus. Fertility treatment is more successful with women than men, and almost nothing can be done if a man cannot produce live sperm. Although the physical problems are shared, emotionally it seems to be women who are most pained by infertility. 'Give me children,' cried Rachel to Jacob in Genesis. 'Give me children, or else I die.'[3] Infertility is not a life-threatening condition, but it's not unknown for a woman to be driven to a suicide attempt.

Kate, 40, had been trying for a baby for three years when she started to get clinically depressed. Her relationship with her husband had broken down because of invasive treatments to the extent that 'the sex act was reduced to something so mechanical, nothing to do with love: I was just going to have some sperm pumped into me.' She says she had no one to talk to, that it became a 'secret problem' and that she retreated further into herself. Eventually Kate tried to commit suicide, using the sleeping tablets that had been prescribed by her doctor, and which she had saved up. I went to bed and thought I wasn't going to wake up again. I wanted to die. There was nothing left to live for.' Fortunately the tablets were not lethal and she was woken four hours later by her husband. 'He was very upset and said "But what about me?" I honestly hadn't thought about him. I'd become totally self-centred: all I could see was my own misery.' Kate rebuilt her marriage with the help of a relationship counsellor, and after six years of unsuccessful treatment eventually accepted the fact that they would not have their own biological children. 'We were emotionally exhausted,' says Kate. They later fostered two young girls, whom they later adopted. Kate tries to explain why she so much wants to be a mother: 'It's the whole thing around being pregnant, giving birth, all the fuss everybody makes of you when you have a child. I did look forward to actually being pregnant, the fertility, the sense that you've got something growing inside you. I've got something in me which is sterile, it hasn't been given the chance to grow and develop. Now I have the girls I don't have to cope with childlessness any more, but I'm still having to cope with infertility.'

A study of married couples found that wives experienced infertility as a cataclysmic role failure, whilst husbands tended to see it as disconcerting, but not a tragedy. Both partners saw infertility as more of a problem for the wife, probably because the expectation to be a father is not as important to male identity as the expectation to become a mother is to female identity.[4]

I was fortunate in being invited to sit in on a meeting of a support group for infertile women who are approaching the menopause. The pain held within the small group of four women was immense, and a sobering contrast to the positive attitudes I had experienced while interviewing many of the women who were child-free by choice. It serves as a reminder that the decision not to have a child is not to be taken lightly. Deeply felt emotions are at stake when we enter the arena of decision-making about parenthood. Here are some extracts from my recordings:

The desire to have children is genetic, as natural as breathing.

I need a baby to give me unrequited love. You don't get that from other people. It's a miracle of creation; it's unbelievable what we're missing out on. I want to experience that, to be given that opportunity. I want a child, even if it was grossly deformed, even if it had only lived an hour. This child that I had produced, the miracle of creation that was mine. I would have achieved something.

It was a way of getting my own identity. I haven't had a child to get my identity through.

I'm not particularly good at painting or whatever, and any other creative area would always be second best to motherhood. It's no good saying develop the other areas and you'll forget the pain.

You have the educational qualifications, are reasonably well off and have everything to give a child, that is the real pain: you've got all that it takes and yet you can't have a baby. It doesn't make sense. When you think of the children born in unfortunate circumstances that have to suffer: those street children in Brazil who don't have a home.

I can't talk to my husband about how I feel. Sometimes the pain is so great, and I think, what's the point of talking about it? It's not going to make it any different. I feel I've let him down, and I've let down his parents as he's an only child. I used to cry at the thought of my husband dying before myself and putting his coffin in the grave knowing he hadn't any children. The meaninglessness of it all.

216

I'm distinctly jealous that men can keep having children right up to their seventies.

For the first eight years of trying for a family I didn't tell a soul. The only person who knew was my husband and the doctors. You can't be seen to be trying for something like that because it's supposed to be something that just happens.

I have to keep working at dealing with it. Something will trigger it off like a friend falling pregnant, or just seeing a baby.

I feel that people pity me. They ask 'Have you got any children?' and I just say, 'No we can't have them.' They don't know how to cope with it. I find I have to say that it's OK, there's no problem. I'm getting on with my life. The pity makes me feel uncomfortable.

At Christmas it's dreadful. It's the worst time of year for me with all the emphasis on television on family life. It's bloody hard sitting there on your own.

You're told that the beauty of not having children is that you can develop other interests. OK, you go along to a group or society, and what happens? They all talk about their children or grandchildren.

Do I really want to be a parent? Despite everything I've been through that question always comes up. There's no guarantee you'll sail through it, and if you didn't like being a mother you couldn't tell a soul.

I can remember I had three embryos put back in, lying on the sofa not daring to move. The thoughts going through my mind were, what am I doing? What happens if I am actually pregnant?

217

We might not have wanted the most prized possession after all, but we didn't have the opportunity to try.

One does wonder how much less acute the pain felt by this support group might be if women were not so specifically defined in terms of their relationship to motherhood; if it were seen more as a particular vocation in life rather than women's entire reason for being. When society tells us from the moment that a baby doll is first put in our hands as a child, that motherhood is what we must expect in our lives, how shattering it must be to discover that fertility is in fact a blessing, and not something we have by right. John Dickson of ISSUE points out that in sex education the possibility of infertility is never discussed. 'People leave school with two messages: we are highly fertile and that we have control over fertility. We're only teaching people one half of the story. Human beings are not very fertile compared to other mammals.' In 1993 ISSUE launched National Fertility Week to highlight the problem of infertility and make people aware that by postponing parenthood, women are gambling with their chances of successfully bearing a child. 'Professional women often go well into their thirties before they even begin to consider having a family,' says Dickson. 'Their most fertile period is late teens, early twenties. If you don't start having children until you're 35 you can run into 40 very quickly.'

Delaying motherhood is in part the reason why both Marina, 51, and Grace, 48, have been unable to have children. Their stories are very different, but they share a similar sense of loss and grieving. There is the loss that their bodies aren't seen to be whole and fully functioning; the loss of an imagined child; and the loss of a longed-for identity. Marina delayed getting married until she was 39. 'I had a lot of catching up to do,' she explains. She comes from a family of two sisters, with a third sister who died before Marina was born. Tragically, her father died of a heart attack when she was 18, just a few months before her younger sister married. Marina felt a strong sense of responsibility to remain in the family home and look after her mother, who had suffered breast cancer before her father's death, and had several relapses in the ensuing years. These emotional difficulties meant that Marina lost several years of education, so she decided to go to university as a mature student and train to become a primary school teacher. In her twenties motherhood wasn't an important issue for her. 'I was a woman coming up to 30, not a maternal woman, never thought of having a baby of my own. I was living my life, getting a professional qualification, and buying a home of my own.' In her thirties Marina had several boyfriends, but 'they never seemed to work out'. Motherhood doesn't appear to have been a major consideration until she accidentally became pregnant at 39. She and her partner planned to have the baby and get married. 'I remember having a bath and thinking, I wonder what's going on inside. I was afraid of childbirth, of bleeding to death and being torn apart, but I never once didn't want it.' When she was eight weeks pregnant Marina miscarried. 'I started spotting and losing blood. We got an ambulance and I miscarried at the hospital. It was incredibly painful physically – it is a form of labour. I remember the nurse offered me a painkiller, and I said no, because of the baby. You do everything to protect the baby.'

Marina went through enormous grief, and became agoraphobic for a short time. She and her partner decided to stick to their wedding plans, and were married six weeks later. Around the time that she and her husband started to try for another baby Marina's mother finally died of cancer. Unable to conceive, the couple went for fertility treatment and had six sessions of assisted conception, one of which was successful. 'People congratulated me. The nurse said don't forget to send us a photograph of the baby when it's born.' Three weeks later Marina had a second miscarriage. 'Physically it wasn't as traumatic, but emotionally it was dreadful. I can remember looking at this stuff in a dish, and it was as though I was looking at a body in an open coffin. I didn't want it to go down the sluice. I realised then that virtually all hope had gone and I wanted to die.'

Much of Marina's need to have a child is about healing her pain and fear of death. 'When you suffer bereavement it's human nature to try and rectify that bad situation. You want to see new life when the old life dies; you need to see renewal. Having children is like being reborn; not having them is genetic death. When we die we won't be leaving anything behind. When I consider my own death I'm frightened. I feel the need to talk to one childless woman who is facing death. How does it feel? What's it like?' Marina is a practising Christian, but her faith has been agonisingly tested. 'I read books written by Christians about childlessness, and they say it's your cross to bear, but I don't go along with that. I have doubted whether there is a God after what has happened to me. I would have thanked God for a child, yet I've been denied that, and all these people who have never even considered God have children. If I were to write a book it would be called "It's Enough to Make You An Atheist".'

Although apparently able to separate female identity from reproduction in her twenties and thirties, Marina now has crippling problems with her sense of self, and with finding a way to live her life meaningfully. She has put much energy into her work, leaving teaching twelve years ago to retrain as a careers counsellor, but Marina finds work a poor creative substitute for motherhood. 'There is nothing on the credit side to make up for not having children. I don't care what people say. They say put your energies into your job, into your relationship with your partner, your pets, holidays. I did those in the past, I will do it in the future, but they cannot compare with being reborn, which is what happens when you have your children.' Marina lives in the suburbs and is surrounded by couples with children. She feels marginalised within her community. 'It must be the same as if you are in a country where you don't belong to the same racial group as the others, or if you're gay and coming out. You feel different. It's almost as though there are physical blows to the chest. It's a pain to go out of the front door – you see people with their baby-buggies and you remember your pain.'

Marina was made redundant a year ago and unemployment further complicates her situation. She is also menopausal, and facing the final loss of hope that she will ever have children (her husband does not wish to adopt or foster). It is an extremely difficult period of her life, and at the time of the interview she admitted to feeling suicidal. 'What is the point of being here?' she cries. 'What benefit am I to society? I don't feel worthy in social terms.' She recognises she is at a major turning point in her life, but as yet has not found a way to accept her infertility, transform the pain and move on. 'I want to

221

WILL YOU BE MOTHER?

move on. I have to make a life for myself.' Courageously trying to work through the darkness, she says: 'I've been given a wisdom, which in a way I'd rather not have. I've known death for as long as I can remember. Perhaps that was God's purpose for me? Perhaps I am changing slightly now. This is my destiny not to have children. Why me? Perhaps that is how Jesus felt – he didn't want to be different. We feel safe in what we know, and we know what we know from our parents. My faith has been severely tested in the past few months, but I think I'm coming around again, slowly coming back to God.'

When I interviewed Grace, she too was at a difficult turning point, approaching the menopause and struggling to finally accept her infertility. Grace had been very involved in left-wing politics and was actively committed to feminism during the 1970s. She has wanted to have a child as long as she can remember, playing with dolls as a small girl and having a fascination with breast-feeding, although there was also an ambivalence: 'I was aware that getting married and having children seemed to be the end of life for women. Children seemed to stop women from doing anything. It stopped them having any kind of life.' Like Marina, Grace was not much concerned with becoming a mother during her twenties. 'Finding myself was important at that time,' she remembers. 'I spent rather a long time in universities, then I got involved in community politics and visual arts. I had lots of relationships and affairs, and seemed to have trouble committing myself.'

When she was 26 Grace accidentally became pregnant while in an unstable relationship with an actor boyfriend. She chose to have an abortion. 'I didn't struggle a lot with the decision. I thought that the child wouldn't stand a

222

chance as I hadn't found myself at all. The boyfriend and I had split up and I didn't think I'd be able to cope. I did grieve. I didn't pretend abortion wasn't death. I think it was a huge thing, but I didn't really work through it, as it involved a lot more self-knowledge than I had at the time. But I did say: OK, I'm not giving birth to a child, so I'll give birth to something else.' Grace vigorously pursued her career as a painter, putting on several exhibitions which attracted good reviews. It was rich, creative period in her life, an abundance of both good and bad experiences. 'It was the birth period of me,' she says. Grace began to have sexual relationships with women, all of which were tempestuous and short-lived. At the back of her mind there was always the question about maternity, and what she was doing about having a child. At 34 she decided to have relationships with men again because her romances with women had been so difficult; also she was now looking for a prospective father.

Grace holds the view that marriage and a stable, committed relationship is not a prerequisite for having a child. She was willing to become a mother alone, although she did want a partner who would be around and play a significant part in the upbringing. In preparation for the prospect of being a single parent Grace decided to train as an accountant, believing it to be a job that would pay her enough to be able to work part-time, continue painting, and raise a child. She also hoped she might meet a suitable partner on the course, but ironically had an affair with a married man who had had a vasectomy. She believes her infertility has been a problem of timing, and that she should have had a child before her accountancy training, which finished when she was 39, despite her fears about being in poverty on social security. She points out that if childcare facilities were better she might have had the confidence to have tried for a baby earlier. 'I shouldn't have been so cautious,' she says.

When 42, Grace joined a dating agency and met her current partner. Unfortunately he has had cancer of the testicles, which affects his sperm count. They agreed that Grace should try sperm donation, but this was unsuccessful. Now, at 48, Grace is on a waiting list for egg donation, but says, 'I feel tired and frightened. I've been struggling with this for thirteen years and it's still not resolved.'

Unlike Marina, Grace moves in a community strongly influenced by feminism where a lot of women have chosen not to have children. 'They believe you shouldn't need a child to be fulfilled. I doubt whether for me work could ever be an alternative or some kind of substitute.' Although knowing so many women without children has been extremely helpful, Grace also says that her friends have not been sympathetic about her desire to become a mother. She has felt a sense of shame at trying so hard to conceive. At the moment Grace's pain about infertility is blocking her artistic creativity. 'As soon as I try to paint I start looking at all the emotional stuff and it's too much. I can't see how to make something positive out of it, it's too painful.' She says that with a child she would feel 'complete' and that 'we would all be here. It feels as if there's something missing. There's an emptiness.'

Transforming the grief

Coming to terms with infertility can be a long and difficult process. Treatments lock couples into a cycle of hope, followed by crushing despair when menstruation starts. Life becomes centred around personal failure rather than achievement. There is no long-term certainty, making it hard to plan ahead. Two out of three women who go for treatments do eventually have a child, but for one woman in three there is no pregnancy. Letting go of the possibility of a child involves a grieving process, often referred to as 'unfocused grief' as it is the mourning of the loss of an experience rather than actual death, and is usually done alone rather than shared. The longer a woman has pursued pregnancy, the longer she mourns her failure to conceive.

Strategies for coping emphasise the importance of once again taking control in life, developing a positive identity and reasserting goals and priorities. One of the infertile interviewees now positively describes herself as child-free rather than childless, and after years of emotional struggle has come to believe in the appropriateness of her life without children. Maureen is now 41 and has been married for twenty years. She and her husband started trying for children when she was 28. 'I didn't get the urge to have them until then,' says Maureen. 'I suddenly felt maternal. All our friends were the same: once one had a baby it triggered the others off. I was also getting fed up with my job working as a solicitor's secretary, but thought what's the point of trying to change, I'm going to have children.' After two months without contraception Maureen's period was late, and her response demonstrates the ambivalence she felt at the time about motherhood. 'I thought, gosh, I'm pregnant. Then I got frightened, and went back on contraception for a little while, for six months. Something inside me asked whether I really wanted this. Then I decided I did and carried on.'

A year later and still with no pregnancy, Maureen and her husband sought medical advice, 'I went in for a laparoscopy and discovered that I only had one fallopian tube. One had disappeared along with my appendix ten years earlier. I also had endometriosis.' Maureen had surgery to try and improve her remaining fallopian tube – but no pregnancy followed. After eight years of unsuccessful treatment it was suggested that they should consider *in-vitro* fertilisation. 'At first I was all for it,' remembers Maureen. 'But then there was a lot of publicity about how stressful it could be and how low the success rate is. I suddenly realised one day that I was quite happy as I was, and if we weren't meant to have children, we weren't meant to have children, and that was that.'

What was behind Maureen's change of heart? She believes the experience of her mother friends had an effect. 'Perhaps I had been looking at motherhood through rose-tinted glasses. When you see the reality of it it's not that easy. I'd seen how some friends of mine who had become mothers had changed. One went from an independent fun-loving woman to someone who lost all her confidence, being at home with children. She worried like mad all the time and all she ever talked about was the children.' Maureen also believes that she and her husband had got used to their lifestyle and would have found change difficult. Deciding not to have IVF was a time to take stock. 'I decided right, I'm not going to have children, what am I going to do with the rest of my life? Nursing had always been on my mind, and when you get to 40 it's either now or never. You've got to make the decision. Was I going to carry on with office work for the rest of my life or not? I decided not.'

Maureen is now studying to be a nurse and says she feels happy and fulfilled. 'I don't think children would have made me happier,' she says. 'It was just this urge that I had. It was a bit like waking up when I suddenly realised that I didn't want them. It was like a cloud had gone for me. I was suddenly me again. It was a tremendous relief to realise that I was fine without children. My life could start again. Looking back now, those ten years seem such a waste.'

Childfree vs. childless

Although infertile women complain that other people display awkwardness in response to their condition, there is at least warmth and sympathy. In contrast, the woman who has no children through choice is often greeted with hostility or incredulity. A few child-free women said that they sometimes deliberately use the subterfuge of infertility because it makes life easier. 'I was sterilised just before my 30th birthday,' says Ilona, 43. She suffers from ulcerative colitis and often uses her illness as an explanation for the sterilisation. 'People look at you and think how on earth could you get sterilised at 30 without any children? I said it was on medical grounds if I felt I couldn't explain to people. I feel more able to tell people it was through choice as I get older. When you're younger you feel more defensive.'

For women who are married or in stable relationships often others immediately assume that infertility is at root of their child-free partnership. Although they wouldn't lie about the reasons why they have no children, some of the interviewees were content to let this misconception ride. 'I just say I have no children, and I know they assume it's

because I couldn't,' says Lucy. Others were keen to
explain that 'I have no children through choice.'

What might a woman without children through choice,
and an infertile woman have to say to each other? It is
tempting to think that an infertile woman might find some
reassurance in seeing another woman positively embrace
life beyond maternity. Her grief might begin to be trans-
formed as she contemplates a woman who does feel whole
without a child, does have a strong sense of identity and
purpose. And the child-free woman? Maybe the agonies
of infertility would make her think again, and ask herself
once more whether she really doesn't want motherhood.
There are few right answers to be found in this maternal
maze, but it is vitally important that we ask the questions.

9

EPILOGUE:
THOUGHTS FOR THE
FUTURE

Will a greater visibility of women living their lives meaningfully without children lead increasing numbers in succeeding generations to make the same decision? If the predictions published in the *British Medical Journal* prove correct, then yes: up to one in three women in this country will opt to remain child-free.

This is a new phenomenon in the West. Elsewhere in the world women have very different options. In our society, where family planning methods are readily available, it is easy to assume that all women are as fortunate. In a recent British survey carried out by the charity Population Concern, it was discovered that one-third of those polled believed that everyone in the world has access to contraception. 'If only that were true,' says Diana Brown, chairperson of Population Concern. Under half the women of childbearing age in developing countries use modern contraception. In Africa 77 per cent of women who do not want any more children remain without contraception. In Asia the figure is 57 per cent, in Latin America 43 per cent. It is estimated that world-wide birth rates would fall by one-third if all the women who want to limit their childbearing could put this choice into effect.

When thinking of the future it is important to consider the wider issues of overpopulation. 'The fuse of the population bomb has already been ignited and the consequences of the explosion for the future of the world will be a great deal more devastating than any nuclear holocaust,' warns Prince Philip, who is president of The Worldwide Fund for Nature International. The statistics are frightening: the world population has reached 5.5 billion and is set to double by the year 2050. 'If you think it's crowded now, by this time tomorrow a quarter of a million more people will join you on the planet. That's the same as the entire population of London being added every month,' reads a Population Concern advertisement. The consequences for the environment are devastating, as ever-increasing numbers of people plunder the earth's resources and pollute the atmosphere.

When asked about overpopulation all of the inter-viewees said that it greatly concerned them. 'Over-population is an obvious and growing global problem,' says Amelia, who works in environmental protection. 'There is no reason for anyone to have a child just for the sake of it if that child is not 100 per cent welcome, and considering the population problems it is madness to do so.' Says Jane: 'Humans are destroying the world and global overpopulation is the most serious problem. We do hear about a declining birth rate in some Western countries, but you only have to look around to see how overpopulated we are in Britain. In addition, one person here uses many more resources than one in the Third World.'

With a fertility rate currently at 1.8, the long-term population of Britain is in decline: it could be argued that there is a need to sustain the numbers of babies being born. David Willey is chairman of Optimum Population Trust, a voluntary organisation concerned with over-population in Britain and Europe. 'People tend to think that overpopulation is not a problem in Britain, but because of the population structure it will increase until at least 2010,' he says. 'As the standard of living goes up more people have cars and houses with gardens, more people consume more. The number of people you can fit in just goes down. If you go on the Underground in London or drive a car on the M25 it's quite clear.'

It's predicted that the population of Britain will continue to rise from 57.5 million to 60 million. Different indicators suggest enormously variable figures for the maximum carrying capacity of our country. Agricul-turalists argue that our current methods of intensive farming are unsustainable, and that organic farming could support a national population of 50 million. Energy experts argue that if we have to abandon coal and oil, and nuclear energy cannot be utilised safely, renewable energy sources could only support a population of 8 million. Willey believes that a child-free woman in Britain is having more than just a symbolic impact. 'It's far less symbolic than re-using an envelope. The environmental impact of one person in the industrialised world is 30 times greater than one person in the Third World. When a woman in this country has three children, that is like having 90 children. Personally I don't like the idea of saying you can't have more than two children, but I would say think about it and don't listen to people who say it doesn't make a difference or who make you feel there's a moral obligation to have children.'

The decision whether or not to have children is uniquely individual, and results from the coming together of a whole bundle of personal needs. It's hardly surprising that no interviewee had made the private decision not to have children on the very public basis that it would be beneficial to the planet. But the issue of overpopulation does bolster their decision. 'There were many other factors which dissuaded us from having children before we were required to think about the issue of population,' says Karen. The population crisis gives the child-free woman some moral high ground when defending her choice. Says Amelia: 'At least I know I'm not contributing to overpopulation, and I could always give that as an answer to charges of selfishness.' Says Maud: 'I thought to myself, I'm only one, but I can light a candle.'

Rajamani Rowley, director of Population Concern, says that gender equality is a key factor. She cites women's education as crucial, as it empowers them to have a larger say in how they want to lead their lives: 'Most often women are only seen as childbearers and childrearers, and there is very little to take into account what their needs are and what they want.' Perhaps what women most want is the chance to determine their own identities: an opportunity to explore themselves free of gender role constraints. As the new identities of child-free women receive more social recognition and acceptance, perhaps in the twenty-first century we will not think that the woman who does not become a mother has something

232

missing from her life, and that every life path is nothing more than an inferior substitute for motherhood. The space in the child-free woman's life is not empty and barren, but full of potential.

NOTES

Preface

1. *British Medical Journal*, 307, 30 October 1993.
2. I use 'childless' if it was the word used by interviewees, book extracts and so on.

1 You *will* be mother: the social pressures to have children

1. Jacqueline McGuire, 'Sons and Daughters', in Ann Phoenix, Anne Woollett and Eva Lloyd (eds), *Motherhood: Meanings, Practices and Ideologies*, Sage Publications, London, 1991.
2. Nazer, 1974, quoted by Joseph Chamie, *Religion and Fertility: Arab Christian–Muslim Differentials*, Cambridge University Press, Cambridge, 1981.
3. Piux XII, 1958, quoted by Joseph Chamie, *Religion and Fertility*.
4. Genesis 1: 28.
5. See Joseph Chamie, *Religion and Fertility*.
6. Kathy Merlock Jackson, *Images of Children in American Film*, Scarecrow Press, Metuchen, New Jersey and London, 1986.
7. Margaret Walters, in the *Listener*, Vol. 120 22–9 December 1988.
8. Marcia Pally, 'Kin Con', *Film Comment*, Issue 1, Vol. 24, February 1988.
9. Suzanne Moore, in the *Guardian*, 4 June 1992.
10. Sigmund Freud, *New Introductory Lectures in Psycho-analysis*, vol. 23 of James Strachey (ed. and transl.), *Standard Edition*, Hogarth Press, London, 1974.
11. Judith D. Schwartz, *The Mother Puzzle*, p. 63, Simon & Schuster, New York, 1993.

2 Pregnancy and the maternal instinct

1. Sheila Kitzinger, *The Experience of Childbirth*, Penguin Books, Harmondsworth, 1967.
2. Edward Shorter, *A History of Women's Bodies*, Allen Lane/Penguin Books, London, 1983.
3. Adrienne Rich, *Of Woman Born*, p. 51, Virago Press, London, 1976.
4. Simone de Beauvoir, *The Second Sex*, p. 514, Penguin Books, Harmondsworth, 1972.
5. John Nicholson, *Men and Women: How Different Are They?*, Oxford University Press, Oxford, 1993.
6. J. Money and A. Ehrhardt, *Man and Woman: Boy and Girl*, Johns Hopkins University Press, Baltimore, Maryland, 1982.
7. Mardy Ireland, *Reconceiving Women: Separating Motherhood from Female Identity*, Guilford Press, New York, 1993.
8. De Beauvoir, *Second Sex*, p. 501.
9. Elisabeth Badinter, *The Myth of Motherhood*, p. 81, Souvenir Press, London, 1980.
10. Nicholson, *Men and Women*.

3 The mother experience

1. Julian Hafner, in *The Times*, 31 March 1993.
2. Elisabeth Badinter, *The Myth of Motherhood*, Souvenir Press, London, 1982.
3. Suzanne Moore, in the *Guardian*, 29 January 1993.
4. Paula J. Caplan and Jane Price Knowles (eds), *Motherhood: A Feminist Perspective*, Haworth Press, New York, 1990.
5. Jane Price, *Motherhood: What It Does To Your Mind*, Pandora, London, 1988.
6. Stephanie Dowrick and Sibyl Grundberg, *Why Children?*, The Women's Press, London, 1980.
7. Helen Franks, *Mummy Doesn't Live Here Anymore*, Doubleday, London, 1990.
8. 'I Wish We Never Had Our Child', *Marie Claire*, June 1992.
9. Susan J. Creighton, *Child Abuse Trends in England and Wales 1988–1990*, NSPCC, London, 1992.
10. Estela Welldon, *Mother, Madonna, Whore: The Idealization and Denigration of Motherhood*, Free Association Books, London, 1988.
11. Jacques Lacan.

12. John Cleese and Robin Skynner, *Families and How to Survive Them*, Methuen, London, 1983.
13. NSPCC, Market Research for the Act Now for Children Campaign, 1992.
14. Caplan and Price Knowles (eds), *Motherhood: A Feminist Perspective*.
15. Price, *Motherhood: What It Does To Your Mind*, Pandora, London, 1988.
16. Brigid McConville, *Mad to be a Mother*, Century Hutchinson, London, 1987.
17. Jean Veevers, *Childless by Choice*, Butterworth (Canada), Ontario, 1980.
18. Song of Solomon 8:6.

4 Making the decision

1. Mardy Ireland, *Reconceiving Women: Separating Motherhood from Female Identity*, Guilford Press, New York, 1993.
2. Joseph Rowntree Foundation, Housing Research Findings, No. 68, York, 1992.
3. Jean Veevers, *Childless by Choice*, Butterworth (Canada), Ontario, 1980.
4. *Ms*, 3 December 1986.
5. Joan Michelson and Sue Gee (eds), *Coming Late to Motherhood*, Thorsons, Wellingborough, 1984; Penny Blackie, *Becoming a Mother after 30*, Basil Blackwell, Oxford, 1986.
6. Estela Welldon, *Mother, Madonna, Whore: The Idealization and Denigration of Motherhood*, Free Association Books, London, 1988.
7. Shere Hite, 'I Hope I'm Not Like My Mother', in Jane Price Knowles and Ellen Cole (eds), *Motherhood: A Feminist Perspective*, Haworth Press, London and New York, 1990.
8. Adrienne Rich, *Of Woman Born*, Virago Press, London, 1976.
9. Hannah Gavron, *The Captive Wife*, Routledge & Kegan Paul, London, 1966.
10. Nancy Friday, *My Mother, Myself*, Fontana, London, 1988; Nancy Chodorow, *The Reproduction of Mothering*, University of California Press, Berkeley, 1978.
11. Ann Snitow, 'Feminism & Motherhood: An American Reading', *Feminist Review*, Spring 1992.
12. Germaine Greer, *The Change*, Hamish Hamilton, London, 1991.

13. Boston Women's Health Collective, *Our Bodies Ourselves*, Penguin Books, Harmondsworth, 1973, 1989.
14. Robyn Rowland, *Living Laboratories: Women and Reproductive Technology*, Lime Tree, London, 1992.
15. Peter Honey, in Vale Marriot and Terry Timblick, *Loneliness: How To Overcome It*, Age Concern, London, 1988.
16. C. Wenger, *The Supportive Network: Coping with Old Age*, Allen & Unwin, London, 1984.
17. D. Jerrome, 'Intimate Relationships', in J. Bond and P. Coleman (eds), *Ageing in Society*, Sage Publications, London, 1990.
18. David Weeks, *Loneliness in Old Age*, Abbeyfield Society, Hertfordshire, 1992.

5 Contraception choices and abortion

1. Simone de Beauvoir, *The Second Sex*, Penguin Books, Harmondsworth, 1972.
2. Mary Boyle, 'The Abortion Debate: A Neglected Issue in Psychology?', *The Psychologist*, March 1993.
3. Gerald Worcester, in *Doctor*, 14 March 1991.
4. W.F. Hendry, 'Vasectomy and Vasectomy Reversal' in M. Filshie and J. Guillebaud (eds), *Contraception, Science and Practice*, Butterworth-Heinemann, Surrey, 1990.
5. G. Howard, 'Who Asks for Vasectomy Reversal and Why?', *British Medical Journal*, 14 August 1982.
6. J.P. Calvert, 'Reversal of Female Sterilisation', *British Medical Journal*, 17 January 1987.
7. Germaine Greer, *Sex and Destiny: The Politics of Human Fertility*, Secker & Warburg, London, 1984.
8. B. Thompson *et al.*, 'Some Factors in the Choice of Male or Female Sterilisation in Aberdeen', *Journal of Biosocial Science*, 23, no. 3 (1991).

6 Child-free women and their relationships

1. Joan Chandler, *Women without Husbands*, Macmillan, London, 1991.
2. Michael Argyle, *The Psychology of Happiness*, Routledge, London, 1989.

3. Gilbert Tordjman.
4. John Nicholson, *Men and Women: How Different Are They?*, Oxford University Press, Oxford, 1993.
5. Helen E. Fisher, *Anatomy of Love*, Norton, New York, 1992; Liz Hodgkinson, *Happy to be Single*, Thorsons, London, 1993.
6. Liz Hodgkinson, 'Leave Us Alone', the *Guardian*, 25 January 1993.

7 Work and the leisure lifestyle

1. Equity and Law Survey: 'Bringing up Baby', June 1993.
2. National Council of Women of Great Britain Survey: 'Project Women', September 1992.
3. Mardy Ireland, *Reconceiving Women: Separating Motherhood from Female Identity*, Guilford Press, New York, 1993.
4. Susan McRae & W.W. Daniel, *Maternity Rights in Britain*, Policy Studies Institute, London, 1991.
5. Institute of Manpower Studies, *Beyond the Career Break*, IMS Report 223, London, 1993.
6. Judith D. Schwartz, *The Mother Puzzle*, Simon & Schuster, New York, 1993.
7. Ann Snitow, 'Feminism and Motherhood: An American Reading', *Feminist Review*, Spring 1992.
8. Jean Veevers, *Childless by Choice*, Butterworth (Canada), Ontario, 1980.

8 Infertility

1. Sheila Kitzinger, *Women as Mothers*, Fontana, London, 1978.
2. Germaine Greer, *Sex and Destiny: The Politics of Human Fertility*, Secker & Warburg, London, 1984.
3. Genesis 30:1.
4. A.L. Griel, T.A. Leitko and K.L. Porter, 'Infertility: His and Hers', *Gender and Society*, 2, no. 2 (1988).

Index

INDEX